COMMUNITY WORK WITH MIGRANT AND REFUGEE WOMEN

COMMUNITY WORK WITH MIGRANT AND REFUGEE WOMEN

'Insiders' and 'Outsiders' in Research and Practice

AUTHORED BY

NAOMI THOMPSON
Goldsmiths, University of London, UK

With

RABIA NASIMI
University of Cambridge, UK

MARINA ROVA
Goldsmiths, University of London, UK

And

ANDY TURNER
Goldsmiths, University of London, UK

emerald PUBLISHING

United Kingdom – North America – Japan – India
Malaysia – China

Emerald Publishing Limited
Howard House, Wagon Lane, Bingley BD16 1WA, UK

First edition 2022

Reprints and permissions service
Contact: permissions@emeraldinsight.com

British Library Cataloguing in Publication Data
A catalogue record for this book is available from the British Library

ISBN: 978-1-80117-479-4 (Print)
ISBN: 978-1-80117-478-7 (Online)
ISBN: 978-1-80117-480-0 (Epub)

Printed and bound by CPI Group (UK) Ltd, Croydon, CR0 4YY

ISOQAR certified
Management System,
awarded to Emerald
for adherence to
Environmental
standard
ISO 14001:2004.

ISOQAR
REGISTERED

Certificate Number 1985
ISO 14001

INVESTOR IN PEOPLE

While we were finishing this manuscript in summer 2021, the Taliban seized power in Afghanistan.

One of the authors of this book was a child refugee; her parents fled the Taliban in 1999 and arrived in the UK in a refrigerated container with their young children.

This book is dedicated to all the women who have had to live in fear, surrender their freedom, or flee their homes and countries – to those who stayed and those who escaped, to those who survived and those who tragically did not.

CONTENTS

LIST OF FIGURES

ABOUT THE AUTHORS

Naomi Thompson is a Senior Lecturer in Community and Youth Work at Goldsmiths, University of London. She is a sociologist of community, faith and inclusion. She is an applied researcher with a focus on co-production and on ensuring the voices of marginalised and excluded communities are heard.

Rabia Nasimi is a former Afghan refugee who fled Afghanistan in 1999. Whilst studying Sociology, she was extensively involved in running a refugee community organisation, a charity founded by her father to support refugee integration in the UK.

Marina Rova is a dance movement psychotherapist and lecturer. She is programme convenor for the MA Dance Movement Psychotherapy programme at Goldsmiths, University of London.

Andy Turner has worked for over three decades in community and youth work, living and working in some of the poorest parts of England as a practitioner, manager, researcher, trainer and activist. He is a lecturer and programme convenor for the BA Social and Community Work at Goldsmiths, University of London.

ACKNOWLEDGEMENTS

We would like to thank all at Emerald involved in the commissioning, publishing and editing process – Iram, Kim, Kirsty, Amber, Brindha, Hayley, Gabriella, Helen, Shanmathi and David – and others behind the scenes whose names we may not have heard.

We owe thanks to the Pilgrim Trust who funded the women's project and the accompanying research over three years.

We are very grateful to the director, staff and volunteers who were part of the community organisation in which the research that underpins this book took place. We are not listing names in order to help protect the anonymity of the women's project and the women who engaged with it – but we are immensely thankful to all in the charity who supported the project and the research study over the three years, of which there are many. Thank you also for your tireless work supporting our refugee and migrant communities in London and beyond.

Naomi would also like to thank all the family, friends and colleagues who have supported and encouraged her to complete this book – of which there are too many to name them all. She would particularly like to thank her partner, Steve, and son, Dylan, for their constant love, support and encouragement. She is also very grateful to the women in her life who have taught her about inequality and courage and who have informed and shaped her own understandings – including, among many others, Rachel McRobbie, Funke Abimbola, Dawn Bowman, Vicki Waddingham, Lara Pereira, Charlie Porter-Baker and Živilė Stanton.

Thanks from Rabia: I would like to give a thank you to my family for their love and support. I am eternally grateful for the opportunity my family and I have been given to migrate to the UK for a better life, and the love and support we have received whilst living here.

Marina would like to thank the women who attended the creative workshops for their generosity of spirit in sharing their stories and supporting others during the process. Marina is also indebted to the women who have shared in her own story of becoming, as a cultural nomad and immigrant to the UK, and wishes to thank her DMP sisters Davina Holmes and Nanette

Hoy and her ArtsMinded sisters Claire Burrell and Marika Cohen for being a constant support and source of inspiration.

Thanks from Andy: For Eve, Millie, Jess and Rach – my clan who bring adventure and love. For mum – a counsellor at Coventry Refugee and Migrant Centre working with refugees and asylum seekers in areas of torture, loss and bereavement – for all your work, inspiration and love.

Finally and most importantly, we would all like to offer our gratitude and admiration to all the women who shared their stories – without you this book would not exist.

1

INTRODUCTION – INTERSECTIONALITY, INTEGRATION AND EMPOWERMENT

This place means freedom to me because my husband didn't let me go to college, but I explained there are no men here... I travel over an hour on the bus even if I'm ill... I've sometimes felt depressed because of my illness as well but when I'm here I forget all the pain and I'm happy. I don't even know how the day is passing so quickly when I'm here. All I've done for six years is walk to the nursery and school and back but now there is something different.

(Mariam, women's project participant)

Mariam's statement that 'This place means freedom to me' represents the powerful impact of community work with some of the most marginalised groups in society. Mariam's story, before engaging with the women's project, is of a woman who had been several years in the United Kingdom but not yet learned English or made steps towards integration beyond taking her children to school and nursery. She was unable to communicate with their teachers about her children's education – or speak to her doctors about her health problems, without a family member or an interpreter present. She felt almost completely isolated. Other women in our research reported similar experiences of never having been able to shop alone, use public transport, learn to drive, or access services. Many did not socialise outside of their immediate families. Few of them took time to focus on themselves. One small grassroots community project became a place of freedom and empowerment for these women where they developed social solidarity, knowledge and resources, set goals for their lives and became both more aware of the inequalities they face and more able to stand together to overcome them.

The women's project coordinator described a situation where many of the women 'bring their four walls of isolation with them' when they settle in the United Kingdom and at their point of first contact with the project (see Chapter 5). Some women were living with husbands and families that were complicit in their isolation. However, societal prejudice, structural discrimination and cultural insensitivity had largely compounded the isolation of the women, particularly when they had made attempts to 'integrate' or to access services or support. These challenges meant the women in our study often lacked a means of survival, or even any small part of their lives and identities, that was independent of their immediate families. Such freedoms need to be articulated as fundamental *rights* for all women and not simply *privileges* for some. Policy and practice need to focus on protecting these basic human rights for refugee and migrant women (often a hidden and isolated group) and within this, to support them to overcome their isolation.

At the time of writing, a renewed humanitarian crisis is underway in Afghanistan, the country where around half of the women in our research were from, as well as being the country from where one of the authors of this book fled the Taliban with her family as a young child. A new UK resettlement programme is in place for displaced people from Afghanistan, a country where women and girls in particular are facing new challenges to their rights, freedoms and safety. This makes ever more pertinent the need to consider how we can effectively support marginalised refugee and migrant women to be empowered and fully integrated in their communities and society, taking account of their needs and assets, recognising the traumas they have experienced and the strength they hold.

This book offers the findings of our research (undertaken by academic researchers and community development workers) over three years in one community organisation working with marginalised refugee and migrant women. The proceeding chapters explore a community-based, bottom-up approach to engaging with migrant and refugee women, drawing on our case study. The organisation delivers a model of practice that involves accessible and culturally sensitive English language education, practical/informative workshops and social integration in a women-only community space, rather than these elements being accessed separately in formal spaces.

Some in the community development field, both in research and practice, may take issue with our inference that these women are marginalised – due to a turn away from deficit-focused interventions in community development in recent decades (McKnight & Kretzmann, 2012). However, we argue that our research demonstrates that the women's needs and challenges first need to be recognised and responded to, in order to work with their assets and potential. This is particularly important for work with the most marginalised, isolated and traumatised groups. We consider the debates about focusing on assets or needs in Chapter 4 and argue for a balanced approach that is bottom-up and long-term, recognising the detrimental impact of top-down, short-term, deficit-focused policy and practice.

Whilst the women in our research have shown great resilience they have also experienced many traumas, and these require a trauma-informed approach that meets their needs (see Chapter 8). The book argues for a bottom-up approach that centres on needs as well as assets, rejecting the binaries of current practice debates in community development. The research has significance in understanding the importance of grassroots needs-based initiatives for engaging marginalised communities. It highlights the importance of cultural relevance of services and a long-term and holistic approach to integration and empowerment that acknowledges the full range of needs and experiences the women face.

This chapter offers the background to the women's project, within which our research was conducted over three years. It outlines the theoretical frame for the text, which is grounded in feminist intersectionality. It explores key concepts such as migrant, refugee, integration and empowerment and high-lights contested definitions and understandings of these terms. Finally, it pre-sents an outline of the book and what the different chapters will cover.

THE WOMEN'S PROJECT

Our research took place over three years with a women's project delivered by a small London-based charity. The organisation was established in 2001 when its founder, a refugee from Afghanistan who arrived in the United Kingdom with his family in 1999, began organising events and trips for other people from Afghanistan. The organisation has since expanded into a charity that helps refugees and migrants tackle the isolating factors which come with migration. The charity works primarily (but not exclusively) with refugees and migrants from Afghanistan and other Central Asian and Middle Eastern countries living in London, providing a range of services that include English language classes, employment workshops, a legal advice clinic, a children's Saturday school and homework club, youth and family support services, drop-in and telephone support, volunteer placements, and cultural and social events.

The women's project was one aspect of this range of support. For the three years in which our research took place, the project received funding centred on the delivery of monthly workshops on issues relevant to the women's lives (e.g. health, education, rights) and on the provision of one-to-one support for some of the women. However, the provision our research participants were engaging with was much wider than monthly workshops and one-to-one support. Much of the women's project work was delivered 'in kind' and by volunteers. The women's project ran weekly (rather than monthly, as funded) and provided English classes alongside workshops, as well as a range of regular social events, all in a women-only space. Children's classes and homework clubs were also provided during the times that the women's project was running. Many of the women also accessed other elements of the charity's provision such as the legal advice clinics.

The broad aims of the women's project were: firstly, to engage marginalised migrant women, particularly those from more conservative backgrounds or living isolated lives; to facilitate their involvement in practical workshops focused on topics that support their empowerment; to supplement this with individual mentoring support; and, ultimately, to move towards the women running workshops themselves and making broader changes in their lives that support their empowerment and integration. The project worked with both newly arrived women and those who had been in the United Kingdom for many years but had remained isolated over time. This book draws on the research data we collected with the women's project over three years. The study was dominantly qualitative and provided rich accounts of the women's experiences with the women's project over time. More detail on the research approach and methods is provided in Chapter 2.

A THEORETICAL FRAMING IN FEMINIST INTERSECTIONALITY

Feminism and intersectionality provide a theoretical frame for this text. Feminist theory gained prominence in the 1970s to pay particular attention to the structures and divisions of gender in society, in response to the context in which women's voices and experiences were marginalised (and often entirely absent) in traditional and mainstream sociological theory (Cree, 2010). The voices of migrant and refugee women are often still marginalised today in theory, research, policy and practice. For these women, while their gender often exacerbates their marginalisation, other issues such as race, religion, culture, poverty and displacement all contribute to their invisibility and oppression. As such, an intersectional frame allows us to recognise the range of factors that impact on their lives and experiences. Critical race theories emerged at a similar time to feminist theory (Cree, 2010) and are also relevant in this context, again justifying the intersectional approach.

Critical and intersectional feminist and race theories present an appropriate frame because they emerged as a challenge to the marginalisation of both women's and racialised groups' voices and encompass an understanding of other factors that marginalise people. Intersectionality itself emerged from within critical feminist and race theories to recognise how gender and race are intersecting issues that cannot be viewed or responded to separately. In particular, it was developed to make more explicit that the experiences of oppression for Black women are unique and intertwined and cannot be simplistically divided along the lines of race and gender (Crenshaw, 1989).

Kimberlé Crenshaw (1989) argued that being 'Black' and being a 'woman' need to be considered together and not as separate issues for Black women. Coming from a background in law, she argued that legal systems (not just academic theory) needed to recognise how these issues intersect rather than treat them as separate issues of discrimination. She introduced the concepts of *racialised sexism* and *gendered racism*, specific forms of oppression for Black women, that reflect the interactions between the intersections of race and gender and create unique barriers and forms of prejudice. She was interested in how overlapping (minority) social identities relate to systems and structures of oppression. Her theory is now used widely to understand how people face multiple and intersectional discriminations and oppressions.

As such, framing our research in feminist intersectionality allows us to recognise the multiple identities and oppressions experienced by refugee and migrant women. It also emphasises gender as a key issue for these women that exacerbates their isolation beyond that experienced by refugee and migrant communities more broadly. Their isolation and oppression are often compounded from both within and without their communities. The intersectional framing, however, allows us to develop broader intersectional understandings of refugee and migrant women's lives, with potential to understand the complexly interrelated roles of factors such as class and poverty, religion and culture, race and ethnicity, as well as gender.

Our approach to conducting the research is grounded in this theoretical frame as we use qualitative narrative research to draw out nuanced understandings of refugee and migrant women's experiences in their own voices. In their book 'Telling Stories' Maynes, Pierce, and Laslett (2008) advocate for this approach to draw out marginalised voices and to provide counter-narratives, such as those of women in male-dominated institutions. This book is our attempt to present the marginalised voices of migrant and refugee women, who have been neglected in the discourses informing policy, practice and research, including in our field of community development.

We have deliberately not overemphasised the positions of already dominant theorists in community development. Instead, we focus on drawing out newer and more marginalised perspectives that problematise some key assumptions in our field. Our engagement with the community development literature occurs primarily in Chapter 4. However, most prominent and important to the theorising we do in this book are the voices of migrant and refugee women themselves. We hope the women's stories in this book help to shape community interventions with them, and academic discourse about them, and that it contributes to addressing the absence of their voices and experiences in both policy and academic debates in our field.

MIGRANT, REFUGEE OR ASYLUM SEEKER?

Migrant people are categorised in different ways. Labels are often applied by others, through policy definitions, from the outside – and contribute to the 'othering' of migrant and refugee communities, particularly where they are bound up in problematic discourses about them.

In the UN's 1951 Refugee Convention, a refugee is defined as 'someone who is unable or unwilling to return to their country of origin owing to a well-founded fear of being persecuted for reasons of race, religion, nationality, membership of a particular social group, or political opinion' (UNHCR, 2021a). However, whether someone is considered a migrant or refugee has become increasingly defined by the host countries, with governments and their agents reserving the right to decide whether the person's 'fear' is 'well-founded' or not. Right-wing governments and populist calls to become tougher on migration mean such decision-making processes have been changeable over time.

In the current context, United Kingdom and international policy retains the right to determine whether someone is legitimately a refugee or not. Governments have implemented processes of deciding whether someone will be granted 'refugee status' after they seek asylum in a particular country. As such, prior to their application being successful, they are considered by policy to be an 'asylum seeker' rather than a refugee (Refugee Action, 2016). Even whether someone can legitimately be considered for asylum is bound up in complex rules around when and where the individual first claims asylum after their displacement, during their migration journey and/or after arrival in the United Kingdom.

As such, an 'asylum seeker' is defined by policy as someone whose asylum claim has been submitted and is under consideration, whereas someone with 'refugee' status is a person within the first four years of a successful claim (Taylor, 2009). Following this, they can apply for 'indefinite leave to remain' but rights to family reunion remain restricted until a person is granted 'exceptional leave to remain' (Taylor, 2009). As such, a person's status as asylum seeker, refugee, or citizen is entirely validated by the host country (in this case, the United Kingdom) and not the individual.

Asylum seekers in the United Kingdom are not allowed to gain paid employment, but they can claim a restricted level of welfare and healthcare (Taylor, 2009). Those refused asylum lose this limited access to support though they retain very limited access to urgent healthcare if and while they remain in the country. These people whose claims have been refused may be deported or become undocumented migrants without recourse to public funds, unable to gain legitimate employment and living in fear of deportation. The UNHCR (2021b) emphasises that when a person is refused asylum, it does not mean that their claim was 'bogus' or 'illegal' and argues they should not be framed or treated as criminals. Despite this, over the year ending in March 2021, the United Kingdom entered almost 13,000 asylum seekers at various stages of their claims into detention, and this was a 44% reduction on the previous (pre-pandemic) year. While this figure represents the number of entries into detention over a one-year period, there were a total of 1,033 individuals in detention at the end of March 2021, and this was also lower than pre-pandemic figures (UNHCR, 2021b).

In addition to refugees arriving in the United Kingdom and seeking asylum after arrival, some refugees are proactively brought to the United Kingdom through resettlement schemes, though these schemes settle relatively small numbers of people overall (UNHCR, 2021b). Recent examples include the schemes for vulnerable persons from Syria (for refugees fleeing ISIS) and Afghanistan (for refugees fleeing the Taliban).

The broader term, migrants, is used to refer to both economic and undocumented migrants – as well as often, erroneously, also for those who have fled to the United Kingdom for safety, creating the sense of a homogenous group of alien invaders that seek to benefit from UK society. Populist fears about exaggerated influxes of economic migrants are often conflated with fears over arrivals of asylum seekers, as seen in the Brexit campaign when the UK Independence Party's poster contained an image of a line of non-European refugees, confusing migration from the European Union (EU) with those seeking asylum from other countries and continents. Grouping all migrants together in media and populist discourse, whether asylum seekers and refugees or not, serves to purposefully disregard their reasons for migration. Banded together, these migrants are viewed as a burden on welfare and the taxpayer and/or as 'taking jobs' from British people (Philo, Briant, & Donald, 2013). This is despite limited rights to welfare and to gaining employment, particularly while seeking asylum or, even more so, after an application is refused (Taylor, 2009).

In a climate of increasing right-wing populism, those risking their lives to seek safety are often referred to in derogatory ways. For example, they have been referred to as 'terrorists' and 'cockroaches' by public media in recent years (United Nations Office of the High Commissioner on Human Rights, 2018). Such framings are racialised and serve to criminalise those fleeing harm. Overall, the terms and categories relating to migration have arguably become 'othering' definitions, often framed in negative ways and used to distinguish between who is a 'legitimate citizen' and who is an outsider. This is reinforced in policy, media and populist discourse.

INTEGRATION (AND IDENTITY)

Shaping positive identities and facilitating integration are key government priorities for marginalised and migrant groups who are settled in the United Kingdom (Home Office, 2015). However, evidence suggests that developing a positive sense of identity and engaging with communities and society can be particularly challenging for many migrant communities. Hall (1995, p. 8) argued that identities 'actually come from outside, they are the way in which we are recognized and then come to step into the place of the recognitions which others give us'. This creates a conflict between internal identification and external grouping, particularly when negative labels are present, such as those associated with migrants, in the current global context of political populism.

Rostami-Povey (2007, p. 241) found that women from Afghanistan displaced to the United States and United Kingdom were 'constantly engaged in mediating between Western values and their Afghan/Muslim cultural identities'. Similarly, Mandaville (2009) argued that Muslims in Europe with transnational identities are viewed with suspicion. This clash of identities affects not just migrant groups but Muslim groups more broadly. For example, UK research has found that both migrant and British-born Muslims perceive a tension between their identities where they feel that society wants them to choose between being Muslim *or* British (Ahmed, 2015; Casey, 2016).

Policy approaches to integration reinforce this identity clash (Haverig, 2013; Kortmann, 2015). Haverig (2013) argues that since 2001, policies have been driven by a fear of migrant communities and often Muslim communities in particular. Integration policies over recent decades have tended to focus either on multi-culturalism and creating cohesion through celebrating diversity, or on acculturation and requiring migrants to assimilate to their host culture (Haverig, 2013; Kortmann, 2015). Based on research with migrants in the Netherlands and Germany, Kortmann (2015) challenges this binary and argues that integration policies need to allow both for migrants to retain their religious, ethnic and cultural identities as well as to make some adaptation and be included in the host culture. UK integration policy has shifted sharply towards the acculturation form of integration since 2010, with its focus on conformity to a vaguely articulated set of 'British values' (Home Office, 2015).

Viruell-Fuentes, Miranda, and Abdulrahim (2012) outline how a sole focus on the need for acculturation obscures the structural factors that compound difficulties faced by migrant communities. Through focusing on perceived cultural dissonance (and indeed cultural differences) of the migrant group, policy can effectively obscure how society reinforces the intersectional discrimination, marginalisation and other problems faced by migrant groups.

Arguably, conceptions of integration have been dominantly framed in othering discourses. Narrow policy definitions of integration can serve to emphasise the outsider status of those whose intersectional religious, racial, cultural and other identities do not reflect the norm for what is considered to be 'British'. This is reinforced in research, as demonstrated by some of the studies outlined above where groups were found to feel under pressure to choose between national, religious and other identities (Ahmed, 2015; Casey, 2016; Mandaville, 2009; Rostami-Povey, 2007).

Alternative definitions of integration frame it as more than merely acculturation, suggesting it is a two-way process. Valtonen (2004) recognises the need for those who are required by their new countries to integrate, to also maintain their own identities that reflect their lives and cultures to date. She defines integration as 'The ability to participate fully in economic, social, cultural and political activities without having to relinquish one's own distinct ethnocultural identity and culture' (Valtonen, 2004, p. 74). This definition recognises the intersectional experiences of migrants and how these will continue to shape their identities post-migration. This more nuanced understanding of integration as a two-way process has been embraced, at least in theory, by policy in Scotland. The 'New Scots: Refugee Integration Strategy 2018 to 2022' defines integration as 'A long-term, two-way process, involving positive change in both individuals and host communities, which leads to cohesive, diverse communities' (Scottish Government, 2018, p. 10). Such conceptions of two-way integration processes place responsibility not just on the individual but on the society and communities they are becoming part of.

This reflects a progressive approach to integration in devolved Scottish policy. However, such a definition is not popular among conservative governments and is not adopted by English or UK-wide policy. The Conservative-led government since 2010 has focused primarily on people's conformity to 'British values', a shift away from New Labour's focus on multi-culturalism. Such policy that reinforces people's 'otherness' and their individual responsibility to conform has dominated in an increasing climate of right-wing populism that has seen the United Kingdom leave the EU, largely fuelled by fear of migration.

EMPOWERMENT

Perhaps more helpful and person-centred than a focus on integration, the broader concept of empowerment frames people's increased participation in their lives, community and society as for the ultimate purpose of achieving greater social justice.

> *Empowerment is a social-action process that promotes participation of people, organizations, and communities towards the goals of increased individual and community control, political efficacy, improved quality of community life, and social justice.*
>
> *(Wallerstein, 1992, p. 1)*

Empowerment is recognised widely as a key value of community development, in literature and practice, as well as by UK national endorsement bodies for the sector (CLD Standards Council, 2021; ESB, 2015).

However, it is also a contested concept within the field, with critiques bound up in questions around who has (or should have) the power to give, thus disputing how far it can be viewed as a means to pursue social justice. It is problematised by those who argue that the notion of workers giving power to others is top-down or even colonial in nature (Belton, 2009, 2017). This reminds us to be wary of how such concepts can be gendered and racialised and to remain reflexive about the dynamics of power between practitioners and the groups they work with, particularly in relation to their intersectional identities and oppressions, ensuring that practice supports rather than obstructs social justice.

Others argue that skilled community development practitioners support marginalised groups to draw out their own power, rather than them being empowered (or given power) by those working with them (Fitzsimons, Hope, Cooper, & Russell, 2011). Sadan (2004) draws on Kieffer's idea that the process of empowerment is usually borne out of a sense of disempowerment: 'The empowerment process in most cases begins from a sense of frustration: people's sense that there exists an unbridgeable gap between their aspirations and their possibilities of realizing them' (Kieffer, 1984, cited in Sadan, 2004, p. 151). As such, it is widely viewed in the field as a process of rebalancing power, particularly for disempowered groups.

From a Foucauldian perspective, marginalised migrant women are a group with little power in influencing discourses about them because of a lack of knowledge and status in the societal hierarchy (Foucault, 1970). In this book, we argue there is a deficit of knowledge capital among migrant women, who lack language proficiency and understanding of UK systems, and that isolation cements this knowledge deficit. As such, they may feel powerless in their interactions with society because of a lack of information and resources to engage successfully.

Powerful global discourses about Islam exacerbate the powerlessness of marginalised Muslim groups in particular (Coppock & McGovern, 2014). Muslim women in the United Kingdom face multiple intersections in their identities leading to multiple oppressions; ethnic, cultured, religious and gendered (Thompson & Pihlaja, 2018). For migrant Muslim women from conservative backgrounds, these intersectional oppressions are more pronounced, and their marginalisation can be reinforced by both cultural practices and societal prejudice.

For groups who clearly lack power, such as refugee and migrant women, empowerment may be a transformational process. Such a process needs to be embedded in practices that recognise the inequalities and intersectional oppressions that have contributed to the stripping of power of certain groups in society, as well as how institutions such as governments, media and others are central to marginalising such groups in the first place. As such, empowerment should not only be concerned with an individual empowering themselves but with challenging the structures that reinforce the disempowerment of certain groups.

OUTLINE OF THE BOOK

This first chapter has introduced the book, offered some background to the women's project that formed the case study location for our research, presented our theoretical frame in feminist intersectionality and introduced key concepts and their underpinning tensions.

Chapter 2 outlines the research approach and explores the value of insider research when working with marginalised groups, outlining how the research involved project staff and volunteers working alongside the external researcher to help gather the research data. It explores the need for reflexivity in research and considers the positionalities of researchers and notions of power in research.

Chapter 3 presents contextual information on migrant and refugee communities in the United Kingdom and also provides contextual data on the specific community of women who used the women's project, including demographic details and characteristics as well as additional details such as levels of literacy. The chapter draws on both secondary literature and primary data from the project.

Chapter 4 presents a literature review that offers a critical analysis of community development practice in the austerity era and how it relates to community engagement with migrant and refugee women. The chapter explores the current context of disparate and under-funded practice, and the need for bottom-up engagement with refugee and migrant women, drawing on key debates in community development such as those relating to focusing on assets vs. needs and on bottom-up vs. top-down practice. It argues for a bottom-up approach that focuses on both needs and assets so that women's needs are not ignored and they are empowered to draw on their own potential in responding to them.

Chapter 5 presents the thematic findings from the first year of the research. The key themes that emerged related to the women's happiness and well-being, confidence, knowledge and skills, integration, freedom and empowerment. The chapter considers how change began to occur in the first year of the project through sustained engagement and positive relationships between the women and project staff and volunteers. However, this change was more aspirational than tangible in the first year of the project.

Chapter 6 presents the thematic findings from the second year of the research. The key themes that emerged related to the women feeling safe, reducing their isolation, building positive relationships, living healthy lives, learning English, accessing services and engaging with their children's schooling. The chapter outlines how the impacts in the women's lives moved from being largely aspirational in year one to becoming more concrete year two.

Chapter 7 provides case studies of women's empowerment gathered towards the end of the third year of the women's project. It demonstrates the grassroots nature of the women's project in that women who engaged over time often became volunteers or even staff. It demonstrates the importance of long-term engagement with vulnerable groups in that empowerment and change in the women's lives became more sustainable over time. It also recognises the impact of disruption and precarity in community work with refugee and migrant women.

Chapter 8 explores the need for a trauma-informed approach in work with women from refugee and migrant backgrounds who may have experienced multiple traumas including displacement, isolation, violence and abuse, and health trauma, among others. The chapter explores experiences of trauma that emerged in the narratives of the women over the three-year project and the themes that emerged from a pilot of creative 'body and mind' workshops in year three that drew on movement and art therapy methods.

The final chapter draws out the key implications for policy, practice and research from across the text and argues for an integrated model of practice for community work with refugee and migrant women. It outlines the challenges to successful engagement with refugee and migrant women that emerged in the research. It develops a model of long-term empowerment that illustrates the process observed in the women's project case study over time and that has potential for wider application. It brings together the key arguments of the book and explores how they might be applied to research and practice with migrant and refugee women as well as other marginalised groups.

2

INSIDERS AND OUTSIDERS IN RESEARCH WITH REFUGEE AND MIGRANT WOMEN

This chapter presents the methodology that we employed in our research with the women's project and focuses on the value of insider research with marginalised groups. Refugees and migrants are often treated as 'outsiders' by society, and scholars have argued that gaining their trust in research is a sensitive process, particularly where they have experienced trauma and/or come from war-torn countries.

We begin with an outline of the research approach and methods before we present an overview of relevant literature on insider research, reflexivity and community-based participatory action research. Within this, we consider the power dynamics of involving insiders in research with marginalised groups. In our main discussion, we (Thompson and Nasimi) consider our positionalities as researchers on the project and the impact our levels of insider and outsider status had on the research. Through our discussion, we demonstrate how the nuances and fluidity between our statuses as insiders and outsiders were both helpful, and at times inhibiting, to the research.

Our analysis adds further nuance to previous discussions of insider research and particularly the rejection of the insider/outsider binary, through considering the levels of insider and outsider status inhabited by researchers and the fluidity between positionalities. We consider the different levels of 'insider' and 'outsider' status that researchers can take on and the overlaps between these – for example, in terms of gender, culture, ethnicity and status within the organisation, reflecting our own intersectional identities. We reflect on the power dynamics and implications of being fluid and partial insiders and outsiders in both research and practice.

Our consideration of our fluid status as *insiders* and *outsiders* in the project recognises that these are not fixed or absolute positions. However, we argue that some level of 'insider' status is needed in effective research and practice with marginalised groups. As a grassroots project that was led by 'insiders' from refugee backgrounds themselves, the women's project was able to create safe spaces for both practice and research – and these are inextricably linked.

THE RESEARCH APPROACH

The approach to our research was interpretivist, in that we recognised that people cannot be researched in the same way as objects because their opinions, feelings and experiences are central to research about them. Whittaker (2012, p. 9) recognises that the interpretivist 'argues that the research methods of the natural sciences are inappropriate to study social phenomena because they do not take into account the viewpoints of the social actors involved'. Qualitative research from an interpretivist approach recognises that research findings are not widely comparable or generalisable as people are not the same and experience things and respond to experiences differently. As such, we use our case study to provide implications for practice (see chapter nine), but we avoid suggesting that the findings are generalisable to all groups of migrant and refugee women. As such, practice must remain reflexive, participatory and open to the views and experiences of those it serves, something we found to be crucial in this study.

In line with the interpretivist paradigm, our research methods were dominantly qualitative. However, we also gathered a small amount of contextual quantitative data (particularly around the demographics of the groups of women who were part of the research). Our aim was to conduct qualitative longitudinal research that took an *ethnographic* approach as far as was possible, that is to study people in their naturally occurring settings (Denscombe, 2007). In this case, this meant that the researchers would be with the women in situ, in their engagement with the women's project. The use of insider researchers, alongside the external academic researcher, supported this approach. The qualitative methods included observations, case studies and reflections, as well as interviews that took the form of open and informal conversations during visits to the women's project. Quantitative data was gathered via registration forms completed with the women when they first attended the women's project and through evaluation forms used after project workshops took place.

The research employed Qualitative Longitudinal Research (QLR), exploring women's experiences of the project over three years. Wenham (2015, p. 45) argues that QLR 'enhances our understanding of the dynamics of … people's lives, and crucially, the processes attached to social inclusion or marginalisation'. She draws on her own research with young mothers to demonstrate how the longitudinal nature of the approach allows for an understanding of people's feelings and experiences that goes beyond an isolated snapshot:

> *A young woman who has just found out she is pregnant may feel very differently to a young woman who has come to terms with, and learnt to skillfully and confidently respond to, being a parent. A snap shot picture from a moment of potential crisis or anxiety may lead to a very different judgement of a … person's capacity, resilience and potential than an understanding of them over time.*
>
> *(Wenham, 2015, pp. 45–46)*

Wenham argues that QLR provides a holistic picture that shows how people's experiences change through time. She draws on Neale and Flowerdew (2003) to demonstrate how it also allows for a consideration of how structure and agency interplay in these experiences:

> *…it is through time that we can begin to grasp the nature of social change in their personal lives, and the ways in which structural change impacts on the lives of individuals. Indeed, it is only through time that we can gain a better appreciation of how the personal and the social, agency and structure, the micro and macro are interconnected and how they come to be transformed.*
>
> *(Neale & Flowerdew, 2003, p. 190)*

This is highly relevant for exploring the experiences of marginalised groups such as refugee and migrant women, as well as for considering the kinds of community development practices that support them to navigate their lives, including overcoming both individual and structural challenges, over time. Whilst we were not able to interview all of the same women each year in our research, due to fluctuating attendance at the women's project, the longitudinal approach provided a clear narrative of how the impacts on the women's lives developed and changed over the three years and how they became more empowered over time.

RESEARCH METHODS AND IMPLEMENTATION

The project employed an external academic researcher (Thompson) who worked with the charity's staff and volunteers to undertake the research. The academic researcher began by immersing herself in the project by observing sessions and meeting with staff, volunteers and project participants before working with them to develop and refine bespoke research and evaluation tools. The academic researcher visited the project regularly, and data were gathered over the three years from registration forms from participants, workshop evaluation forms, goal setting exercises and interviews. Project staff and volunteers also provided reflections and case studies from their interactions with the women. The women who attended the project were supported by staff and volunteers to complete evaluation forms after workshops. After the early visits to the project by the academic researcher, the women's project staff and volunteers led the regular collation of workshop evaluation data. The bespoke evaluation form was developed, tested and refined with the women.

Project participants, staff and volunteers took part in interviews. These were qualitative narrative interviews that engaged with broad questions about the women's (and staff and volunteers') experiences of the project and its impact on their lives. Staff and volunteers were also asked about the impacts they observed the project having on its participants. There was also space for the women to talk about their lives more broadly, beyond the women's project. In year one, 15 women took part in interviews. These were with nine project participants, five volunteers and the project coordinator. In year two, seven of the women's project participants, who had attended for at least six months, took part in interviews while project staff and volunteers submitted reflections and case studies. In year three, 15 interviews took place with six project participants, four staff and five volunteers. In year three, several staff and volunteers who were interviewed were also former participants so these interviews covered overlapping roles in the project.

The research obtained ethical approval via the Research Ethics and Integrity Committee at Goldsmiths, University of London. Consent to participate in the research activities was embedded into registration forms as an opt-in question for the women who participated in the project. This covered registration data, workshop evaluations, observations, case studies and interviews. Even after giving this broad consent, the women had the choice to opt out of completing evaluation forms at individual workshops if they wanted to. The interviews with project participants were constructed around broad open questions and were facilitated by the academic researcher with the help of an interpreter from the organisation's staff or volunteer team. These interviews were not audio-recorded but notes were taken by the researcher. Women who took part in the interviews were offered the choice to do so before they were taken aside by the researcher. Information about the study and the women's consent were re-confirmed verbally at the start of each interview, as well as the women being offered the opportunity to ask questions or withdraw. This was more appropriate than providing typed information sheets and consent forms due to the range of languages and low levels of literacy among the women. Separate consent forms were used for interviews with staff and volunteers where these were audio-recorded. All names used in this book are pseudonyms.

INSIDER RESEARCH

As participants with refugee backgrounds may have experienced events and situations where their voices were not respected, it is important to avoid causing harm through doing this in research (Masten & Narayan, 2012). Zulfacar (1998, p. 48) further states that significant importance is given to family privacy and therefore an outsider interfering with this privacy is encountered with distrust. Lipson and Meleis (1989, p. 106) note that suspicion of strangers is common among people from war-torn countries.

Conversely, refugees and migrants are often treated as 'outsider' groups and encountered with distrust by society. This distrust becomes mutual as they are marginalised from services and systems. Insider researchers are important in this context. For example, not just in understanding the participants' backgrounds but in having a more equal and trusted status with participants and being able to effectively communicate about issues of power such as the rights and limits of confidentiality as well as ensuring informed consent and respecting non-consent. Researching *with* not *on* marginalised groups has been highlighted by researchers as an important ethical principle that ensures such groups are empowered rather than exploited (Greenfields & Ryder, 2012).

Post-positivist approaches have been influential in understanding research as partial and subjective and influenced by both the participants and the researcher (Cloke, Crang, & Goodwin, 2005; Rose, 1997). The need to redress some of the power imbalances between researcher and researched led to calls for 'insider' research, which was based on shared attributes (such as language, ethnicity, gender and class) (Merton, 1972; cited in; Botterill, 2015).

According to Horváth, Szakács, and Szakács (2018, p. 7) 'Insider-research means research done by members of the organisational system and communities in their own organisations' and a person can be defined as an insider researcher where they 'possess knowledge, insights and experience before engaging in the actual research'. However, it has also been recognised by Narayan (1993) that insider researchers are necessarily set apart to an extent from other insiders of an organisation or community group through them assuming the status of researcher. This raises questions of power in relationships with other insiders and how fully someone's insider status can remain once they assume the role of researcher. It suggests it is not possible for someone to become a researcher and to also fully remain as an insider.

Following the development of insider research as a distinct methodology, it faced critique from feminist scholars who argued the insider/outsider distinction relies too heavily on binary opposites, or absolute notions of sameness and difference (Rose, 1997). Such scholars argue that the insider/outsider binary is a myth because a researcher's role, position and status is neither impervious nor absolute (Mercer, 2007; Merton, 1972). Intersectional approaches similarly critique the insider/outsider binary, as researchers and participants both engage with and move between multiple positionalities and therefore both may inhibit 'insider' and 'outsider' status at different times throughout the research (Anthias, 2012; Botterill, 2015; Ryan, 2015). We recognise this nuance and complexity in defining ourselves as 'insiders' or 'outsiders' and, through this chapter, we explore further the fluidity between the levels of 'insider' and 'outsider' status that we inhabited in our study.

REFLEXIVITY

There is clearly a need for insider researchers to reflect on and manage the dynamics of power produced by their status. Finefter-Rosenbluh (2017) suggests that insider researchers need to engage in reflexivity in order to ensure they reflect on their own perspectives and biases, draw on more than their own perspective on issues and move beyond commonly shared understandings to draw out the full range of experiences, meanings and interpretations from others inside the organisation or network under study. There is a risk of blurring boundaries of roles and positions which comes with being an insider and of imposing your own values, beliefs and perceptions onto the research participants (Drake, 2010).

It is arguable that researcher reflexivity is needed whether approaching qualitative research with marginalised communities as an 'insider' or 'outsider', as neither position is neutral to power and bias. Reflexivity is defined as the 'active acknowledgement by the researcher that their own actions and decisions will inevitably impact upon the meaning and context of the experience under investigation' (Horsburgh, 2003, p. 309). When researchers and research participants occupy different positions within social structures there is a need to be reflexive about the power dynamics at play. Bourdieu (1996) suggests that researchers may inflict 'symbolic violence' through misunderstanding or misrepresenting research participants and therefore advocates for reflexive practice in research. For both 'insider' and 'outsider' researchers, there is need to 'focus on self-knowledge and sensitivity' and to carefully 'self-monitor' the impact of biases, beliefs and personal experiences on the research (Berger, 2015, p. 2).

PARTICIPATORY ACTION RESEARCH

As Veroff and DiStefano (2002, p. 1192) argue, in action research, epistemological concerns such as: 'what is the relationship between the knower and the known?' and 'how are the researcher and the participants affected by the research?' are focal questions that need to be addressed. Projects which are designed with partnerships of academic and community organisations are vital to foster communication and participation of marginalised groups, as such partnerships mitigate important concerns around power, social relations, participation, learning and community benefit, within research. The involvement of various cohorts of people also helps to facilitate diverse dialogue about social problems.

Community Based Participatory Research (CBPR) is an approach that encourages partnerships between researchers, practitioners and participants in order to develop a clearer understanding of problems and work collectively in order to address them (Israel, Eng, Schulz, & Parker, 2005, p. 3). CBPR contains three main elements, participation, research and action – and involves a systematic investigation of community issues with the aim of education, action or social change (Minkler, 2005). As a form of action research, CBPR involves using partnerships to develop meaningful interpretations of data and test them in the field of action in order to improve a given situation. As such, problem-solving and making change are ontological commitments of participatory action research that entail an active participation of all partners in the process in order to reach these aims.

There is little doubt that research that involves people from different sectors can enhance knowledge about social life (Griffith, 1998). This is reflected in a range of disciplinary areas that have used CBPR as a useful strategy to answer complicated questions such as in health (Israel et al., 2005; Minkler, 2005) and psychology (Jason & Glenwick, 2016; Kloos et al., 2012) among other disciplines. Goodson and Phillimore's (2010) capacity-building research aimed to empower leaders of refugee community organisations. Their methodology centred around providing systematic training for community leaders to act as researchers and to collect robust and reliable evidence. They argued that this process benefitted the community researchers through providing opportunities to learn new skills and work with other groups to deliver a project.

Our own research with refugee and migrant women was participatory to the extent that staff and volunteers helped to shape the research and to collate the data. Many of these volunteers were also project participants that had taken on volunteering roles within the project over time. These staff and volunteers were also research participants. As such, the roles of researcher and participant overlapped substantially. In addition, we developed and changed the research methods and tools over time in response to how they were received by participants and volunteers, including rewriting interview schedules.

The longitudinal nature of the research, over three years, allowed for a process of reflexive adaptation in response to each stage of the process. The interpersonal relations built through such longitudinal engagement can help to overcome power hierarchies, a legitimate concern in any ethnographic study. Here, we argue that a longitudinal and participatory research process helped researchers build trust with community members and to be sensitive to avoiding any misunderstandings or damaging encounters for the already marginalised groups involved. The safety of participants, many of whom had already experienced multiple traumas in their lives, was paramount.

The presence of insider researchers was significant to participants feeling safe. It was also significant to the women's feeling of safety that the community project itself was a grassroots community organisation founded by a refugee family for other refugees and migrants. In the second year of the women's project, 'feeling safe' emerged as a theme from interviews (see Chapter 6). This theme would arguably not have emerged if the practice itself was not provided by insider practitioners nor would the personal examples shared in the research have been shared with a research team of complete outsiders. The women's willingness to engage in research activities was arguably impacted by them feeling safe within the project more broadly. Had they not felt safe, they would have resisted sharing such personal experiences with the researchers.

Through the women's project, the women both experienced the safety of having peer mentors they could relate to as interpreters, workshop leaders and volunteers, as well as having the opportunity over time to take on such roles themselves. This reflects why participatory research was an appropriate method for the project, as it shares similar principles with this form of practice, to provide opportunities for learning, skills development and empowerment (Goodson & Phillimore, 2010).

HOW OUR RESEARCHER POSITIONALITIES IMPACTED ON THE RESEARCH AND OUR INSIDER/OUTSIDER STATUS

On first glance at our status as researchers on the project, it appears that one of us is clearly an external or *outsider* researcher (Thompson) and the other of us is a clear *insider* researcher and practitioner (Nasimi), sharing a similar background with the project participants and working for the charity since before the research took place. However, as we examine in more depth our insider–outsider status, some complexities emerge. For example, despite not sharing ethnic or cultural identities with the participants and having no experience of displacement and migration, Thompson was a partial insider simply because she is woman. It would not have been appropriate or possible for a man to conduct the research because it required entering and inhabiting a women-only space. Through the research, it emerged from some women that they were only able to attend the women's project with the permission of their husbands and this had only been allowed because the women's project was facilitated and attended only by women.

While Thompson was initially very much perceived as an outsider despite being a woman, she became more of an insider over time as she visited the project over the three years and became familiar to the women who attended long term. This process of becoming more of an insider was supported by her delivering a workshop in year two of the project where she shared more about herself which included her connecting with the women about aspects of her life, identity and goals, including becoming a mother at a young age, engaging in study after becoming a parent, and her experience of travel. Her insider status was enhanced in moments she participated with the group but often reverted when she more formally inhabited the role of researcher, when writing notes or conducting interviews, or when longer gaps occurred between her visits. Her outsider status was sometimes a barrier and, at other times, helpful in gathering research data. Her formal status as 'the researcher' made women willing to engage in in-depth conversations with her about their lives and experiences in order to support and advocate for *their* project, particularly when they had to leave an activity such as an English class or workshop temporarily in order to do so.

The presence of insiders (staff or volunteers) to act as interpreters in interviews may have at times limited what women reflected back about the women's project. A desire to please those offering the service led, in year one of the evaluation, to women struggling or refusing to answer a particular question in interview: 'what would you change about the women's project?' Despite this reluctance to respond to this question, women would often approach Thompson later more informally with suggestions for improvement, such as more structure to the childcare or consistency in the English teachers. It appeared that they were uncomfortable making these suggestions when directly asked what they would like to change, and this may have been partially due to the presence of a project 'insider' in the interviews. However, it was only through reflexive conversations with such insiders that the question was adapted to 'what would make the project even better?' A question phrased in this way would typically be avoided in research due to its leading nature. In this context, however, it allowed the women to overcome a cultural barrier to being seen to criticise those who are helping you, something Thompson was naïve to before such insider conversations. Migrant and refugee communities may also be reluctant to be seen to criticise the country or society that has 'accommodated' them, as doing so is perceived by them as making them appear ungrateful or un-British, or feeding already negative discourses about them (Ahmed, 2015). As such, the presence of insiders and the trust built with the academic researcher over time were important to the women being open to sharing honest experiences.

Reflexivity in research design was important from the start so that as Thompson engaged with project insiders (staff, volunteers and project participants) she was able to adapt the methods and tools as necessary, such as in the case of the change to the question outlined above. Another example that occurred in year one of the project was that after evaluation forms for workshops were designed and then checked by staff and volunteers, more adaptations were needed after trialling with the women in larger groups. The questions had included some 'before and after' number scale questions designed to measure changes to knowledge, confidence, thinking and behaviours. These questions proved confusing for women with a range of first languages to complete and were adapted to 'yes/no' questions about whether changes to knowledge, confidence, thinking and behaviour around particular issues had taken place as a result of the workshops.

Nasimi's positionality as a second-generation individual from Afghanistan with parents that migrated to the United Kingdom while she was a young child, as well as being a woman in her mid-twenties, and a staff member at the charity, will all undoubtedly have impacted how she approached the research as well as the knowledge produced from her encounters. Her shared characteristics with the group under consideration allowed her to relate to participants and build a rapport. This insider status as both a researcher and practitioner on the project provided access to isolated parts of the community and an understanding of both the nuances and complex emotions of migrant identity formation. Being part of the group under study means 'simultaneously being an onlooker in the stalls and a member of the cast' (Shaw, 1996, p. 10).

The involvement of staff and volunteers allowed insiders a level of ownership over the research but may have meant that participants assumed the practitioner-researchers were already experts on their lives and potentially led them to hold back elements of their stories when they were present. Botterill (2015) draws on her research with Polish migrants in the United Kingdom, describing how her participants 'took ownership' of the construction of particular narratives. Their enthusiasm in sharing these narratives were intertwined with the assumption that, as someone who was not Polish or a migrant, the researcher lacked knowledge that an 'insider' would have taken for granted (Botterill, 2015, p. 3). Therefore, sharing a similar background with the participants could mean that they might position you as already an 'expert' on their experiences and not share everything it was important to know. Nasimi's status as insider did present a barrier at times; for example, when the participants did not want to be seen to criticise the project and censored some of what they might have said in interviews, when project staff were present.

Knowing that insiders present in interviews also knew some of the people that the participants might reference in their discussion, might also have led to feelings of vulnerability about the information being disclosed. To an extent this was mitigated in this research, as the external researcher led the interviews and as such they might have felt more open to go into detail about their experiences. However, the presence of an interpreter in the room may have perpetuated a feeling of vulnerability/exposure at times. Despite this risk of exposure, the presence of an insider in interviews appeared to increase the comfort to speak overall, with the exception of when the participants had potential critiques to share about the project. This discomfort in these moments potentially exposes the limits of Nasimi's insider status, in her role as a senior member of staff in an organisation providing a service to the women taking part in the research, and the power imbalance this brings. This power dynamic was more equalised when the insiders present as interpreters at interviews were volunteers who had been project participants themselves in the recent past.

This raises questions as to what extent Nasimi could claim insider status. Her position in the organisation gave her a level of authority as did her status as a co-researcher, setting her apart from the research participants (Narayan, 1993). The imbalance of power that such authority in the organisation brings means that participants' desire to please or to 'say the right thing' may have impacted on interviews where she was present, as in the example of the question about what participants would change about the project. When such questions are being asked, not having an insider present, may respond more effectively to issues of power. There are also ways that Nasimi and Thompson were insiders in different ways, at different times and with different women. For example, Thompson had the shared experience of being a mother with many of the women and informal conversations about this enhanced her insider status at times. Nasimi, by contrast, was younger in age and shared many characteristics in common with the women who were not married or who did not have children. Overall, however, Nasimi's experience of arriving in the United Kingdom with her family at a very young age to seek asylum gave her trusted status and shared understandings with participants and allowed her to have insider status as both a practitioner and researcher on the project, which was crucial to the effectiveness of both. As at least a partial insider at all times, she could be an effective mediator between the women and outsiders, enabling them to trust Thompson (the external researcher), for example, when she first introduced her to the project and its participants.

Despite the benefits of being part of the community the researcher wishes to explore, there is also a risk of blurring boundaries by imposing the researcher's own values, beliefs and perceptions as well as the projection of biases (Drake, 2010). This may have been what participants feared in the moments they chose to hold back. Nevertheless, it is important to acknowledge that 'no research is free of the biases, assumptions, and personality of the researcher and we cannot separate self from those activities in which we are intimately involved' (Sword, 1999, p. 277). The question is then how Nasimi used her experience to offer deeper understandings of the phenomenon, without imposing her experience on the participants (Pillow, 2003). This required a level of reflexivity in considering how interviews might best take place. As such, she purposely engaged in activities such as listening more than talking and acting as interpreter rather than interviewer. This arrangement meant that participants could feel comfortable talking with someone they knew well as an insider, whilst understanding that they needed to tell their whole story for the external researcher to understand. The adaptations we made to research tools and interview schedules from the start of the project as we engaged with insiders demonstrates how reflexivity was crucial to all phases of the research process from the formulation of research questions, to collection and analysis of data, and the drawing of conclusions (Bradbury-Jones, 2007; Guillemin & Gillam, 2004).

CONCLUSION

Overall, while we had previously identified ourselves as either insiders or outsiders in relation to the research, through reflexivity over time, we came to understand that we were insiders and outsiders to different extents at different times. Our level of insider and outsider status was based on how far our own intersectional identities (in terms of gender, class, ethnicity, religion, parental status, status and role within the organisation, views and ideologies, etc.) overlapped with those of the women we were engaging at different times. While we are both women, holding roles with authority such as project leader and researcher meant we were at all times, to some extent, apart (Narayan, 1993). This was important to recognise in order to reflect on the power dynamics at play in the practice and research of the project.

Understanding that there was fluidity between our positionalities as insider and outsider enabled us to utilise moments of shared understanding, while remaining reflexive about our role and influence on the research, as well as to understand when our insider and outsider status was helping or hindering the study. Intersecting factors such as our gender, age, language, marital and parental status, as well as our role in and relationship to the organisation all impacted on the research. The use of some participatory research methods allowed us to draw on the insider status of project volunteers and participants to play a role in refining the research methods and as interpreters in interviews.

We argue that understanding the nuances in our status as insiders and outsiders was crucial to the research – rather than these being viewed as absolutes. We suggest that some level of 'insider' status is needed in effective research and practice with marginalised groups, whilst the involvement of partial outsiders alongside can also be helpful. Careful thought is needed as to what would not work along this insider–outsider spectrum – with the poles being necessarily avoided. For example, in the case of this research, a non-female researcher would have not been able to penetrate the safe women-only space, nor would it have been appropriate to do so. However, claiming full insider status between the project and research participants and their insider practitioners and researchers would also downplay that power dynamics are still at play in such relationships of status and that require consistent acknowledgement and reflexivity. Researching others necessarily brings power into play regardless of the researcher's status beforehand.

The qualitative findings that emerge from the research are presented primarily in chapters five to seven, with one chapter for each year of the three-year study. The next chapter (3) explores the context for migrant and refugee groups in the United Kingdom, as well as presenting quantitative data relating to our research participants including demographics, literacy levels and starting points for the groups of women who engaged with the women's project.

3

MIGRANTS AND REFUGEES: AN 'OUTSIDER' GROUP?

This chapter presents contextual information on migrant and refugees in the United Kingdom including data around asylum claims, experiences before, during and after arrival in the United Kingdom, as well as access to assessments and support, and ESOL (English for speakers of other languages) courses in particular (as learning English is identified as fundamental catalyst to empowerment for migrant groups). This chapter also presents contextual data on the specific community of women who used the women's project including demographic details and characteristics as well as additional details such as levels of literacy. The chapter draws on both secondary literature and primary data from the project. The primary data presented in this chapter were gathered from registration forms of the women attending the women's project. In addition, broader data from the charity's ESOL classes are used to provide a snapshot of the literacy levels and educational needs of women who engaged with the charity as well as the flexible and holistic approach to provision that was developed.

The data presented in the chapter illuminate the challenges faced by migrant and refugee groups in the United Kingdom. It outlines how asylum processes alongside patchy provision and support (informed by largely right-wing policies) compound isolation and provide a challenging context for these groups to navigate on arrival in the United Kingdom, providing barriers to their engagement and empowerment in their new communities and society. Migrant and refugee groups experience traumatic trajectories before, during and beyond their displacement, including in their engagement with services and systems after arrival in their new country.

Many of the women attending the women's project were from cultures, countries or communities where illiberal cultural practices are strongly entrenched. Some of these women were new to the United Kingdom and others had been in the United Kingdom for several years but remained isolated. A large proportion (around half) of these women were from Afghanistan, reflecting the origins of the charity and its founders, alongside other women from a diverse range of other (predominately Muslim) countries of origin. The cohort was made up of women who were (or had been) migrants, refugees and asylum seekers.

SEEKING ASYLUM

The United Kingdom takes in a relatively low number of refugees compared to other countries in Europe with similar or lower populations, particularly Turkey, Germany, France and Sweden (UNHCR, 2021c) though the scale of populist, media and political moral panics often masks this. The United Kingdom currently receives around 30,000 asylum applications per year, with a significant proportion of these relating to family groups rather than individuals. Typically, over half of initial decisions on these applications are refusals.

In the year ending June 2021, the United Kingdom received a total of 31,115 asylum applications (this related to 37,235 people, including spouses/dependants of the main applicant) (Home Office, 2021). Of these asylum applications, 2,756 were from unaccompanied children (Home Office, 2021). In the year 2020, the United Kingdom received 29,456 applications for asylum. This was down 18% from 35,737 in 2019, which had been the highest for three years (Refugee Council, 2021a, p. 1). Of applications for asylum made in 2020, 54% of initial decisions were refusals, 40% were granted asylum, 3.8% were granted Humanitarian Protection or Discretionary Leave, and 2% were granted leave to remain under other categories, including 'family or private life' (Refugee Council, 2021a, p. 2).

The decline in asylum applications in 2020 was partly due to the Covid-19 pandemic, when international travel was disrupted. Resettlement schemes were also paused between March and November 2020. In total, only 661 people were granted protection through resettlement schemes (separate to asylum-seeking applications) in the year ending June 2021, down 81% on the previous year (Home Office, 2021). This figure does not include the settlement of people from Afghanistan via a separate scheme for staff and their families who have supported British military efforts in the country, through which 3,300 people were settled in the United Kingdom from 2013 until June 2021 (before the situation escalated in Afghanistan in summer 2021) (Home Office, 2021). In June 2021, delays to asylum application decisions had created a backlog of 70,905 people waiting for an initial decision with 76% (54,040) waiting more than 6 months (Refugee Council, 2021b).

The largest numbers of asylum applicants arriving in the United Kingdom in 2020 and given refugee status or other forms of leave to remain were from Iran, Eritrea, Sudan, Syria and Vietnam. Alongside this were a significant proportion of applicants from Pakistan, Albania and India who received above average refusal rates, particularly from India (Refugee Council, 2021a, p. 10). Of asylum applications in 2020, 22% were from women, slightly below the average for recent years (Refugee Council, 2021a). The refusal rate for women is lower than for men (demonstrated across the data from 2018 to 2020) (Refugee Council, 2021a, p. 3).

As noted in Chapter 1, around half of the women attending the women's project were from Afghanistan. Migration from Afghanistan to the United Kingdom peaked between 1994 and 2004 (Change Institute, 2009, p. 25) and continued steadily thereafter; many fleeing the Taliban. Most migrants and refugees from Afghanistan settled in London, and west London in particular (Change Institute, 2009). Afghanistan has remained in the top ten UK asylum applicant producing countries over the last decade (Refugee Council, 2021a). In the year ending June 2021, over 3,000 of UK asylum seekers were people from Afghanistan (Home Office, 2021). Worldwide, people from Afghanistan were the third largest group of refugees in 2020 (UNHCR, 2021d). As we write, a new humanitarian crisis is underway in Afghanistan (following the withdrawal of US and UK troops after 20 years – and the Taliban once again seizing power in the country). A new UK resettlement scheme is in process – meaning a significant rise in new arrivals from Afghanistan since the data explored here was produced.

TRAUMATIC TRAJECTORIES – BEFORE, DURING AND AFTER ARRIVAL

Unsurprisingly, mental health problems are common among asylum seekers and refugees and at a higher prevalence than in the general population (McManus, Bebbington, Jenkins, & Brugha, 2016). Around one in three refugees and asylum seekers are known to experience depression, anxiety, or post-traumatic stress disorder (PTSD) and this doesn't account for hidden mental health issues among these often-marginalised communities (McManus et al., 2016). The stress, anxiety and increased risk of mental disorders may be rooted in conflict and violence from before the departure from home – a relevant example of this for our study, is of women in Afghanistan, where 46% of women were found to have experienced gender-based violence (International Rescue Committee, 2020).

A study by US organisation, Global Rights, in 2008 found 62% of women in Afghanistan had experienced multiple forms of violence with 87% experiencing at least one form of physical, sexual or psychological violence, or forced marriage (Nijhowne & Oates, 2008). The same study noted 17% of women in Afghanistan reported sexual violence, 11% had experienced rape and 52% reported physical violence, with 39% stating that during the previous 12-months they had been physically assaulted by their husband. Additionally, 74% of the women had experienced psychological abuse and 59% were in forced (as distinct from arranged) marriages (Nijhowne & Oates, 2008). The study highlights the extreme prevalence of violence against women in Afghanistan (even while the Taliban were not in power).

Within Afghanistan, wide variations of experience were also reported between groups and areas with extremely high levels of certain forms of abuse in some areas or for women from rural or tribal communities. For example, 100% of Kochi women (nomadic groups) living in Kabul reported at least one form of physical, sexual or psychological violence and 43% of women in Kandahar reported sexual violence. The vast majority, 92%, of women in the eastern province of Khost were found to have experienced forced marriages (Nijhowne & Oates, 2008). Certain factors amplified the risk of violence – including women being in a forced marriage, being in a polygamous marriage, being under 15 years of age and married, having rigid expectations of gender roles and living in rural communities or in the southern and eastern border provinces. Finally, the study highlighted that an experience of one form of violence increased the likelihood of women experiencing other forms of violence. Protective factors ameliorating risk to some extent included the employment status of both women and their husbands – along with the literacy of both women and men (Nijhowne & Oates, 2008).

Alongside harrowing experiences prior to departing from home, additional distress may be endured as part of the journey to the United Kingdom via land, air and/or sea. This may involve travel through war zones, hostile physical environments, mountain or desert regions – and navigating the risk of being kidnapped, trafficked or facing torture for ransom (UNHCR, 2019). On arrival, separation, discrimination, exploitation and the challenge of navigating a complex bureaucratic system in a new host country and society may intensify initial feelings of trauma. One example is the UK government's own policy of detaining asylum seekers in Immigration Removal Centres and

Short-Term Holding Facilities. Evidence shows that detention adds to the trauma already experienced by the people being placed there (von Werthern et al., 2018). During the year from April 2020 to March 2021 there were almost 13,000 entries into UK immigration detention and this was substantially lower than pre-pandemic levels (44% lower than the previous year) (UNHCR, 2021b).

Refugees may be afraid for family and friends back home. Other concerns may include inadequate housing, or finding ways to integrate, managing extensive isolation, and unemployment (Priebe & Giacco, 2018). Alongside this, refugees are required to go through complex legal procedures as part of claiming asylum status and acquiring permission to remain in a country. Here, significant additional stress and anxiety may be experienced as part of the process of waiting on consideration from the Home Office (Priebe & El-Nagib, 2016; Sijbrandij et al., 2017).

Additional challenges confront minority groups including women, minority ethnic groups, and disabled and LGBTQ + people once located to the United Kingdom, all relating to experiences of oppression, hostility and exclusion. The context for asylum seekers on arrival and as they work to build their new lives is complex, confronting significant challenge including ongoing management of trauma, isolation and financial hardship.

SEEKING ASSESSMENT AND SUPPORT AFTER ARRIVAL

Despite the significant probability of distress, anxiety and mental health impacts (McManus et al., 2016; Public Health England, 2019), the context for UK asylum applicants is one of minimal welfare provision or state-aid. Asylum seekers receive some limited government support for living costs, significantly less than an unemployed UK citizen receiving welfare (Taylor, 2009). An undocumented migrant or person refused asylum has no access to welfare and is unable to open a bank account or find employment.

In the United Kingdom, refugees and asylum seekers often rely on assistance from the voluntary sector – including community organisations and charities. Taylor (2009, p. 770) recognises the critical role of 'the voluntary sector and support networks' in supporting migrant and refugee women in particular but that this can only happen 'where such support exists'. This highlights the important role of grassroots practice – as well as that a reliance on voluntary sector services creates patchy and inequitable provision. In a devolved United Kingdom, health provision is also patchy. Additionally, health providers are subject to regulation to ensure they check patient eligibility – and that they apply restrictions for failed asylum seekers or undocumented migrants who, in England, are charged for non-urgent secondary care. Taylor (2009) argues against this forced and unethical role for healthcare practitioners in enforcing immigration policy.

Complicated admissions procedures and protracted waiting times become obstacles to refugees and asylum seekers accessing support more broadly (Gateley, 2015, p. 38). For those arriving after a more prolonged experience of trauma, an assessment of support needs becomes more urgent. In the early 2000s, a UK Government report emphasised the importance of in-depth assessments that are sensitive to the newly arrived person's particular needs (DfES, 2003). More recently, Doyle and O'Toole (2013) reached similar conclusions based on interviews with refugees and service providers – and argued specialist staff are essential in providing suitable assessment for newly arrived people. Creating effective and meaningful methods of assessment that identify the full range of support needs, however, has remained a challenge (OECD, 2018).

A further concern is that after assessments have been undertaken, limited public funding means that services offering advice and support are limited, particularly holistic and longer-term provision (Gateley, 2015, p. 42). The impact of trauma is often overlooked in the services that are available, which focus narrowly on integration. The challenges marginalised migrant women, in particular, face in accessing services are explored further in Chapter 4 and the need for trauma-informed practice is explored further in Chapter 8.

LEARNING ENGLISH, FINDING EMPLOYMENT AND (DIS)EMPOWERMENT

Learning to speak English has been identified as crucial to migrant groups becoming less isolated and more able to integrate (Casey, 2016). Learning the language of their host country is a primary aspiration of migrant people (Ward, 2008, p. 6) with refugees and asylum seekers in significant number seeking access to ESOL classes (UNHCR, 2019). Lack of English language reinforces further the isolation of already marginalised groups of women, who often do not have the same opportunities for integration as the men in their communities (Cheung & Phillimore, 2017). Developing language ability is critical for supporting social and economic integration and to combatting isolation.

Although language acquisition is critical for migran
government funding for ESOL was cut by almost 60% an
million between 2010 and 2016 (Refugee Action, 201⁷
learners are recent immigrants (Ward, 2008, p. 6), of which a
number are refugees (UNHCR, 2019). Even prior to cuts in provision, ESOL
students reported challenges in accessing courses, because classes were over-
subscribed (Dimitriadou, 2004). Current issues include fees to attend classes,
lengthy waiting lists, complicated admissions procedures, students being
assigned to unsuitable classes, and the limited availability of childcare (OECD,
2018; Refugee Action, 2017a, 2017b, 2018). The process of waiting and the
formal and disconnected nature of ESOL provision have been found to amplify
feelings of isolation (Dimitriadou, 2004; Refugee Action, 2017a). ESOL classes
are usually separate from other support services, taking place in formal settings,
requiring consistent attendance and assessment, and not supporting learners
to engage socially with each other.

Asylum seekers and refugee students face significant additional demands,
which may disrupt or block attendance at ESOL classes (Collyer, Morrice, Tip,
Brown, & Odermatt, 2018). These include missing classes and assessments for
required attendance at Home Office interviews and meetings with solicitors.
For women in particular, the cost of registering and travelling to classes and
lack of childcare have been found to be obstacles, preventing access to ESOL
provision (Higton et al., 2019; Phillimore, Ergun, Goodson, & Hennessy,
2007). Mixed gender classes are also problematic for some women. Language
acquisition also correlates with health and employment status – those unemployed due to ill health confront more difficulties acquiring English language
than those in good health and those who are studying, looking for work or
employed. A study of resettled refugees found 22.3% of males and 20.6%
females referred to both poor health and caring responsibilities as obstacles to
their learning – impacting on class attendance and when present, their ability
to concentrate (Morrice, Tip, Collyer, & Brown, 2019).

Levels of pre-migration education are also a significant factor in predicting
the English language acquisition skills for migrants – where little or no pre-
migration education indicates more limited language acquisition capacity
(Morrice et al., 2019). Many refugees and asylum seekers are from countries
where literacy rates are low, particularly for women. For example, in 2010/
2011, Afghanistan had a literacy rate of 22% amongst women aged 15–24
(UNICEF, 2018). In the United Kingdom, these problems are compounded
by a lack of ESOL courses at the lowest entry levels (Stevenson, Kings, &
Sterland, 2017, p. 21). Refugees are most likely to have a very low level of

ᴇnglish proficiency and require beginner level ESOL classes (Higton et al., 2019; Mackey, 2019).

Once attending classes, asylum-seeking and refugee ESOL students may struggle with aspects of programme design and delivery, requiring additional support. These groups may need to gain understanding of particular areas of language quickly, that aren't typically covered in the ESOL curriculum. Simpson (2019) for example, highlights an immediate need for legal language that asylum seekers require to help navigate the legal processes they are subject to. Similarly, Taylor (2009) identifies that a lack of understanding of health jargon exacerbates problems with accessing appropriate healthcare.

There is an absence of universally agreed definitions or models through which the success of ESOL is measured (Klenk, 2017, p. 167). The current emphasis on integration by policy-makers is typically measured by an individual student's engagement in formal employment. In short, paid work has become the tangible outcome measurement (Cooke & Simpson, 2009; Klenk, 2017), which while relevant for some, may not be the intended or actual outcome for many women in migrant and refugee communities. As acknowledged in Chapter 1, the integration policies of successive UK governments have increasingly shifted towards assimilation over the last two decades, where refugee and migrant communities are labelled as an alien 'other' expected to conform and integrate into UK social, cultural, and economic norms. This approach is reflected in ESOL provision where success is measured only by narrowly defined indicators of integration such as gaining paid employment.

Where refugees and asylum seekers can speak a certain level of English, reading and writing skills can be significantly weaker (Nellums et al., 2018a, 2018b), restricting access to further study or employment. Early on in developing new language acquisition, low-income jobs with no interaction with others may slow or halt progression and limit higher-level language development (Morrice et al., 2019). Willott and Stevenson (2013) highlight the significant proportion of refugees who arrive in their new country with professional experience, qualifications and a high level of skills. However, the under-employment of refugees after arrival impacts on their self-esteem and mental health (Bariso, 2008; Salvo & Williams, 2017; Willott & Stevenson, 2013).

All of the issues identified in the literature highlight the need for specialist and holistic provision for migrant and refugee groups, where ESOL classes, employment support and social integration are elements of a range of support services that are sensitive to cultural and specific needs and that recognise strengths, assets and potential. Arguably, policy and practice more broadly could avoid inflicting further trauma by working to a model of integration services that takes a holistic approach to migrant experiences and that does not require them to sacrifice or deny their own histories, cultures and experiences (or their skills and strengths) in order to settle in the United Kingdom and be a full part of society.

THE WOMEN WHO ATTENDED THE WOMEN'S PROJECT – COHORT PROFILE

In year one, the women's project was located in both south-east and west London. In years two and three, the project was primarily located in west London. The sections below draw primarily on the women's project cohort data. In the section on education and literacy levels, we also draw on broader data from ESOL classes that formed part of another project run by the charity. This additional data allow us to develop a clearer picture of the literacy levels and educational needs of the migrant and refugee women who accessed the charity's services. The women's project was attended by 71 individual women in year one, 101 in year two and 68 in year three. The decrease in attendance in year three reflected some disruptions to the project, including a shift from running the project in two locations to one (see Chapter 7).

Countries of Origin

The women's project had particular success in engaging women from Afghanistan, reflecting the background of the founders, the focus of much of their work and where their offices were located in west London. The women's project engaged primarily Muslim women, from a wide range of countries of origin. While a significant proportion of the women each year were from Afghanistan, 33 other countries of origin were represented by the women attending.

In year one, 44% of the women were from Afghanistan with the other 56% from 16 other countries of origin. In the second year of the project, 58% of the women were from Afghanistan with the other 42% from 18 other countries of origin. The higher proportion of women from Afghanistan in year two reflects the relocation of the project to west London where the Afghan population is at its highest in London. In the third year of the project, this balance had shifted somewhat and 50% of the women were from Afghanistan with the other 50% from 17 other countries of origin. Overall, around half of participants were from Afghanistan and half from a range of other (predominately Muslim) countries in central Asia, the Middle East and Africa (such as Iran, Iraq, Pakistan, Syria, Jordan, Egypt and Algeria). A small proportion of attendees were migrants from European countries and an even smaller number were from South America. The cohort, to an extent, reflected the large-scale global population movements, specifically 'Europe's refugee crisis', which peaked in 2015, when large groups of people fled violence in Syria in particular, as well as other countries such as Afghanistan, Pakistan and Iraq among others (Pollard & Howard, 2021).

Age and Family Status

In years one and two of the women's project, the women ranged in age from the early and mid-twenties to the late-forties, widening further in year three to include women aged from 17 to 62 years. Most of the women in years one and two had families and many of them had significant caring responsibilities for their children and extended families. As an example, the number of children the women had in the second year of the project is illustrated by Fig. 1.

In year three, fewer of the women had families than in previous years, though 41% did have children and several of those without children were married and intending to have children. The most regular attendees tended to be those with children who also attended sessions at the charity (homework clubs or Arabic/Farsi language classes).

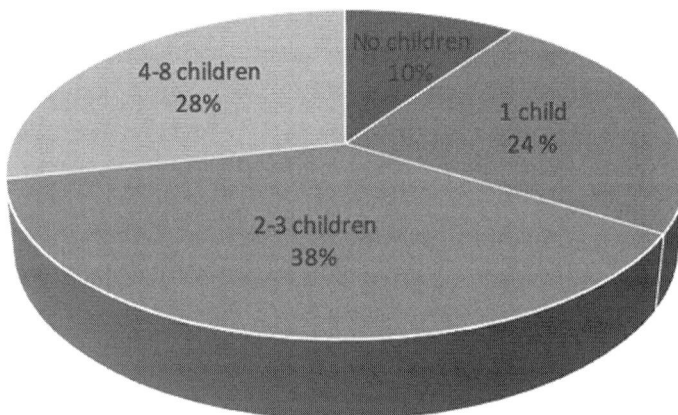

Fig. 1. The Number of Children the Women Attending the Women's Project had in Year Two.

In year three, there were higher levels of literacy among the women. This appeared to reflect, in part, a larger proportion of the women having been younger on arrival in the United Kingdom and without families and therefore more able to focus on their own learning, as well as that some of them had engaged long term and improved their English significantly over time. Older women across the three years often reported they had been in the country several years before finding the charity. Many (but not all) of the younger women tended to be more progressive in relation to their own ambitions and development, and less isolated overall, than the older women who engaged with the project. This is explored further through the qualitative data in Chapters 5, 6 and 7.

Education and Literacy Levels

The previous education levels of the women ranged from no education at all to university degrees. Where they had university education, this was in all cases achieved in their home country in their first language. Even in year three when overall literacy levels were generally higher, 59% had no previous education (with many unable to read and write in their first language) and only 10% had university education. While the women's project did not collect specific data on literacy levels – as the project centred more on the practical workshops than its attached ESOL provision – a separate evaluation of the charity's ESOL classes more broadly did gather such data. Overlapping years two and three of the women's project, two of the authors of this book (Thompson and Turner) were involved with this broader evaluation.

At the start of year three of the women's project, the charity more broadly had a total of 267 students enrolled onto ESOL classes in west, south and south-east London. Classes ran up to three times per week in each area and several of these were women-only classes. Those that were not women-only classes were majority female participants. For example, of 170 people on the enrollment lists for ESOL classes in west London, only 28 were male. Some women were unwilling (or not allowed by their families) to attend classes with men and therefore the women-only classes were crucial for the engagement of several of the women. Women-only ESOL classes ran alongside the women's project as part of the holistic model of provision, and were often the draw for women to engage with the charity in the first instance. The significance of learning English emerges as a key theme throughout the three years of the data (see Chapters 5, 6 and 7).

The significant interest in the charity's ESOL classes is perhaps unsurprising due to the cuts to UK ESOL provision and long waiting lists for classes with formal and statutory providers. The charity's ESOL classes were all either funded by grant-giving foundations or offered 'in-kind'. The women-only English classes attached to the women's project in particular were offered 'in-kind' throughout the three years. This meant that there was, at times, some disruption and inconsistency in the provision of these classes. This reflects the precarity of ESOL funding and provision in the United Kingdom more broadly.

Typically, ESOL classes cover a range of levels of study with each course focused at one level, requiring assessment in order to progress to the next level. Providers assess a student's level of English before assigning them to the appropriate class. There are three 'entry levels' – Entry Level 1, 2 and 3 for students who are not yet ready to study for a level 1 (or higher) qualification. Students who are assessed to be at Entry Level 1, 2, or 3 can move through the entry levels then progress to qualifications at level 1 and above. The charity's ESOL provision attracted students (the majority of whom were refugees) with the lowest levels of literacy – beginner, pre-entry and entry levels. As many of the women were unable to read and write in their first language, the barriers to learning a new one were even greater (Morrice et al., 2019). ESOL classes (and available curricula and materials) had to be adapted to work with students who were not yet ready for Entry Level 1, typically the lowest level of ESOL study.

Data for one west London class revealed just over half the cohort (51%) were at beginner or pre-entry level and a class in south-east London had two thirds (66%) at beginner or pre-entry. Data from the south-east London sample show that the majority of students that undertook assessments did reach and begin to move through Entry Levels 1 and 2. However, progression through the entry levels was more pronounced in speaking than in other areas such as reading, listening and writing. This echoes Nellums et al.'s (2018a, 2018b) finding that many refugees learn to speak English more quickly than to write or read it, reducing isolation to an extent, but preventing access to certain systems and particularly to other courses of study or employment.

Attendance at ESOL classes was fluctuating rather than consistent throughout the year with core groups of regular attendees at classes alongside women who came and went, and often returned later. Staff worked hard to enable new and existing students to join, re-join and participate in the courses throughout the year – and critically in assessments. Of 62 of the charity's ESOL students who took part in a self-evaluation exercise, all identified that their English language skills had improved to some extent. There was also a focus on softer outcomes.

85% associated their improved literacy with feeling more self-confident and 61% reported expanding their social networks through the classes. This demonstrates how a flexible, tailored and holistic approach allows for both confidence and social solidarity to develop for participants.

The participants in the charity's ESOL classes were also involved in goal setting exercises which involved students listing their integration goals. For the south-east London cohort, aside from 'learning English', other goals included 81% of students aiming to 'join a club', 75% 'to join a library', 75% to 'take an IT course' and 54% to 'go to the job centre'. The popularity of joining and attending various services, highlighted the students' focus on 'soft targets', accessing and engaging with key community resources – such as the library or job centre. Here, the data highlight the importance of providing spaces where students could engage in English language acquisition while applying it to the development of broader goals for their lives. A significant minority of students (40%) listed the goal of applying for a job. Overall, the data on integration goals emphasise the complex range of (often subtle) integration outcomes attached to ESOL provision and other integration-related services, challenging the focus on only hard outcomes like gaining employment, particularly for women and the most marginalised migrant and refugee groups.

CONCLUSION

Overall, this chapter has demonstrated how complex legal processes and patchy service provision may compound the isolation, exclusion and trauma experienced by migrant and refugee groups. Statutory processes do not appear to be effectively supporting settlement and integration. For women in partic-ular, hard outcome measures of integration such as gaining employment may not be appropriate. In addition, the problems with service provision prevent marginalised migrant and refugee groups from easily achieving new skills like English language as well as making gains in seeking employment and other integration outcomes. Complex processes and lack of support alongside hard outcome measures and othering discourses may be dis-empowering these groups more than they are supporting their empowerment and integration.

However, women who engaged with the charity in which the women's project is located were able to improve their English, despite starting with very low levels of literacy, often having a low level of education in their own lan-guage as well as in English. The charity's approach suggests a more flexible and holistic model of provision may be more effective, particularly for the most marginalised groups including women from conservative backgrounds.

The next chapter explores further the issues in policy, practice and access to services for migrant and refugee women in particular. It identifies how community development might respond, grounded in debates about top-down versus bottom-up practices and whether policy and practice should focus on the assets and/or needs of marginalised groups.

4

COMMUNITY DEVELOPMENT WITH MIGRANT AND REFUGEE WOMEN[1]

This chapter presents a literature review that offers a critical analysis of community development practice in the austerity era, and how it relates to community engagement with migrant and refugee women. The chapter considers the current context of disparate and under-funded practice, and the need for bottom-up engagement with refugee and migrant women. It draws on key debates in community development such as those relating to focusing on assets vs needs and on bottom-up vs top-down practice. It presents a critique of top-down deficit-focused practice and offers an argument for a bottom-up approach that focuses on both needs and assets so that marginalised migrant women's needs are not ignored and they are empowered to draw on their own potential in responding to them.

The chapter begins with some context on the experiences of Muslim women in the United Kingdom before considering how integration policy is shaped and enacted, calling for a more two-way process of integration to be implemented (as discussed in Chapter 1). It then goes on to consider how top-down mainstream services (that emerge from narrow and populist policies of integration) are failing migrant women and compounding their isolation. It considers how both cultural factors and societal prejudice need crucial consideration in how services are shaped and designed. Research shows that both present a barrier in access to services for migrant women.

---

1 The literature review presented in this chapter is an extended version of the literature review that formed part of a published article: Thompson, N. & Nasimi, R. (2020). 'This place means freedom to me': needs-based engagement with marginalized migrant Muslim women in London. *Community Development Journal.* doi: 10.1093/cdj/bsaa029.

The chapter also considers the key enablers of integration, particularly the need to learn English. This discussion is grounded in recognition of current policy discourses of austerity, division and fear. For example, lack of English language proficiency can be weaponised against migrant groups in policy discourse, despite a lack of government funding for ESOL classes, and alongside the recognition of it as a key need for migrant groups in government-funded research. The chapter considers how community development might effectively respond to the needs of marginalised migrant women whilst avoiding the problems created by top-down policy and practice. We consider possible progressive approaches and alternatives to 'austerity localism' (Featherstone, Ince, MacKinnon, Strauss, & Cumbers, 2012).

Asset-focused forms of community development emerged in Western contexts during recent decades as a form of community self-help, becoming popular in the United Kingdom in early twenty-first century. MacLeod and Emejulu (2014) argue the turn towards interventions focusing on assets rather than needs in community development has cemented neoliberalism, austerity and inequality. Whilst asset-focused interventions are championed as supporting a focus on skills rather than deficits (IDeA, 2010), both the broader literature and our primary research in the proceeding chapters demonstrate the value of also recognising needs of communities, and building on people's strengths to address them. We argue focusing solely on assets would not be as successful in responding to the explicit needs of the most marginalised and excluded groups. We are not suggesting such needs-based interventions need to persistently engage in formal needs assessments – as grassroots bottom-up interventions begin with an understanding of, and sustain an ongoing engagement with, the community being served.

MUSLIM WOMEN IN THE UNITED KINGDOM

Almost half of Muslims living in England reside in the 10% of the most deprived local authorities, and Muslims are more likely to live in poverty than any other religious group (Ali, 2015, p. 46). Poverty and disadvantage are factors for migrants and refugees in particular (Mulvey, 2009). Whilst not specific to migrants, Ali's (2015) analysis of census data found Muslim women in the United Kingdom are less likely to be in employment than women from any other faith group. For Muslim women who are married, this difference is even starker. A significantly higher proportion of Muslim women are looking after home and family as their main occupation (17.8%) in comparison with women from the general population (5.7%) as well as those from other religious groups (e.g. Hindu 8.5% and Sikh 6.4%) (Ali, 2015). Ali outlines this

> ...may be due to the younger age distribution of the Muslim community resulting in higher fertility rates as well as the increased likelihood for Muslim households to be those with dependent children.
>
> (2015, p. 63)

Ali recognises that, whilst for many married Muslim women 'family responsibilities take priority', those who seek work don't get the support they need from existing employability programmes and experience issues such as a lack of flexible working and childcare options, as well as discrimination (2015, p. 63). Similarly, Taylor (2009) argues that employment programmes for migrants tend to neglect women. Ali argues that migrant Muslim women require tailored services to meet their unique needs. She also recognises that some of these women face cultural resistance from their husbands or families to becoming integrated (Ali, 2015). Additionally, there are issues where employment is used as the key measure of integration. For Muslim migrant and refugee women, employment outcomes may either be irrelevant to their lives or particularly challenging to achieve.

Muslim communities and individuals face increasing prejudice in society and institutions, and this prejudice is often gendered (Casey, 2016). This reflects global discourses about women and Islam, with prejudice increasing since 9/11 and with the growth of far-right populism in Western countries (Thompson & Pihlaja, 2018). A number of studies have highlighted the prejudice experienced by Muslim women in the United Kingdom. Nurein and Iqbal (2021) highlight the complex, intersectional identities of Muslim women, finding that racism, gender discrimination and religious discrimination intersect, for Black Muslim women in particular, in a range of services and institutions (Nurein & Iqbal, 2021, p. 434). They argue for a particular need for more representative mental health services, which they find to be currently failing to work effectively with these women, and highlight an urgent need for 'more Black counsellors and psychologists' (Nurein & Iqbal, 2021, p. 445). Similarly, Taylor (2009) highlights how racism and discrimination in health services impact on migrant groups' ability to access and engage with support, particularly for women. He argues there is a need for training for practitioners in healthcare and other agencies in 'cultural, religious and gender sensitivity' (p. 770).

Research has also found mainstream education to be a site of prejudice for Muslim women who report experiencing differential treatment in further and higher education settings. The National Union of Students (NUS, 2018) found that Muslim students are often subject to more scrutiny than others, particularly those active in student unions, international students and women who wear religious attire. Their experiences of prejudice were enacted by both staff and students. The report found Muslim students feared being abused in their place of study with one third stating they had experienced some form of abuse or crime. This prejudice was gendered with female students who wear religious dress feeling most threatened (NUS, 2018, p. 18). This is reinforced by Thompson and Pihlaja (2018) who found female Muslim university students in London and Birmingham identified a link between wearing religious dress and the likelihood of being stigmatised. The institutional hostility and prejudice were highlighted by all these studies as being exacerbated by the UK government's own policies and rhetoric, for example the 'Prevent' programme, enabling discriminatory surveillance and sanctioning Islamophobia (Nurein & Iqbal, 2021; NUS, 2018; Taylor, 2009; Thompson & Pihlaja, 2018).

ENABLING TWO-WAY INTEGRATION

We argue in this book that policy and practice need to develop models for integration services that take a holistic approach to migrant experiences and that do not require them to sacrifice or deny their own histories, cultures and experiences (or their skills and strengths) in order to settle in the United Kingdom and be a full part of society. Chapter one identified an alternative, more mutual process of integration that focuses on migrants' 'ability to participate fully in economic, social, cultural and political activities without having to relinquish one's own distinct ethnocultural identity and culture' (Valtonen, 2004, p. 74). Such an approach allows for a 'long-term, two-way process, involving positive change in both individuals and host communities, which leads to cohesive, diverse communities' (New Scots Integration Strategy, 2018–2022, p. 10).

However, as acknowledged in Chapter 1, definitions of integration that focus on assimilation are dominant, particularly among right-wing governments. In the United Kingdom in particular, there is support among populist groups for punitive approaches to migration, as seen in the popularity of campaigns behind the Brexit vote, such as that promoted by the UK Independence Party (UKIP) which included a poster campaign showing a long line of (non-European) migrants with the term 'Breaking Point' alongside. Similarly, it can be observed in more recent attempts by the UK Home Secretary to change maritime law to allow often-dangerously full (and unfit for purpose) boats carrying migrants across the English Channel from France to be turned back. This is despite the United Kingdom taking in relatively low numbers of asylum seekers and refugees compared to other European countries (UNHCR, 2021a).

Media discourses fuel fear of migrants and the misinformed assumptions that they all (including refugees) only arrive for economic purposes and that overly liberal policies have led to them becoming a burden on welfare and the job market (Philo, Briant, & Donald, 2013). Political mantras have focused on the need for migrants to conform to a vaguely articulated set of 'British values' in recent years (Home Office, 2015) which has placed pressure on migrant groups in the United Kingdom to relinquish any cultures, traditions or habits that might be perceived as non-British, in order to demonstrate full commitment to being 'truly British'. The role of appearance (such as how they dress and/or their ethnic background) in much of this 'othering' (Thompson & Pihlaja, 2018) means that many migrants can never hope to achieve such vague and lofty standards of 'Britishness'. Intersectional oppressions such as racism, religious hatred and gender discrimination all play into the treatment of migrant groups in society as 'other' and never quite British enough. Such political and populist framings of refugee and migrant communities contain core assumptions about these groups as in deficit (a burden to bear on society) – disregarding their personal histories, validated experience, learning, knowledge and capacity to contribute to the host country, the United Kingdom.

In contrast to processes of assimilation, two-way integration works towards a form of acculturation where the cultural and linguistic identity, and sense of home all held by the refugee are maintained even alongside engaging with new communities. In a context where existing assets – the relationships and networks – have been lost or broken via the experience of forced migration, a new sense of belonging can emerge during resettlement (Berry, 2005). Here, practice which enables the development of social and bridging capital, deepening social relationships, becomes vital for refugees (Klenk, 2017, p. 167). This requires holistic models of practice, which are culturally relatable and accessible for the most marginalised groups and that offer a range of integrated services, recognising the unique and interconnected assets, challenges and needs of migrant groups. Such practices need to recognise the needs of women who may be particularly marginalised and may need tailored support in women-only spaces (Ali, 2015).

ISOLATION VERSUS INTEGRATION

Research suggests that marginalised migrant Muslim women in Britain face isolating factors in their lives (Refugee Support Network, 2012; Stevenson & Willott, 2007), and this is often exacerbated by the language barrier and an absence of peer networks (Harinen, Honkasalo, Ronkainen, & Suurpaa, 2012). For Muslim migrants, the Casey report (2016) found a number of issues reinforce social and economic isolation. She identified tensions between Muslim communities and wider society, finding almost half of UK Muslims faced prejudice and over half of the wider public believed there is a clash between British values and Islam. Whilst Casey found, overall, that Muslims feel positive about being British, some women were held back by illiberal views and practices stemming from gendered-cultural traditions. Whilst this moral judgement needs some unpacking, it is reinforced by other research.

Research commissioned by the Department for Communities and Local Government found several barriers to accessing services for women from Afghanistan including a lack of English language proficiency, resistance from their families and negative responses and attitudes from services themselves (Change Institute, 2009). The research suggests public authorities exacerbate the problem by failing to effectively address the challenges women face and that 'misplaced political correctness or cultural relativism' means some decisions made are even harmful (Change Institute, 2009, p. 34). High levels of poor mental health as well as particular challenges in escaping domestic violence were reported among women by the research, as well as ineffective services to respond to these issues, with many mental health problems being missed by statutory health providers for example. The women are described as having a 'relative invisibility' when it comes to statutory services (Change Institute, 2009, p. 34). Similarly, Mirza (2010) has argued that young Muslim women may be let down by services where professionals' attempts to appear tolerant lead them to not follow up on issues of concern, such as around forced marriage, female genital mutilation and other abuses.

Casey (2016) is clear in her recommendations that increasing scrutiny of Muslim communities will not encourage integration. Arguably, there is a need for community initiatives that understand the views and practices of these communities to provide non-threatening services that provide appropriate education and challenge where necessary. Casey's recommendations identify English language proficiency as a key enabler of integration. Paradoxically, for marginalised Muslim women, a lack of English often prevents integration, but their isolation prevents them overcoming the language barrier. Additionally, as highlighted earlier in this chapter, experiences of prejudice are widely reported by even non-migrant Muslims accessing mainstream education (NUS, 2018; Thompson & Pihlaja, 2018). Cultural choices such as wearing religious dress were found to be a key factor in such discrimination. This reinforces the need for the most marginalised groups to be able to access targeted services that are culturally sensitive, meet their needs and deal with the challenges they face. Further, a recognition is needed of how mainstream services and broader society compound isolation, rather than the responsibility for successful integration being placed solely on the migrant groups. This reflects the need for two-way integration services.

EXCLUSION FROM SERVICES

Migrant Muslim women face barriers when attempting to access a range of services. A report exploring the experience of migrants from Afghanistan in West London found that, of council services, most women were only aware of housing and their overall impression was negative (Social Policy Research Centre, 2014). Experiences included having no one get back to them after making a query, and rude and intolerant responses. There were experiences of cultural insensitivity; for example, arriving at a leisure centre's women-only swimming session to find a male lifeguard on duty (Social Policy Research Centre, 2014). The report found women engage more positively with services where long-term contact can be made with specific people rather than one-off fragmented interactions with different people and providers.

In academic research with migrant women in the United Kingdom from Africa and Asia, Giusta and Kambhampati (2006) found that close proximity to their ethnic communities alongside contact with their host communities contributed to feeling settled. However, experiences of services like housing and immigration could impact negatively on them feeling settled. This has implications for the need for culturally appropriate provision for migrant women. In particular, provision to support their English language learning and access to wider services in a women-only space over a long-term period. Mainstream services are not effectively meeting the needs of marginalised Muslim women and this increases their isolation rather than facilitating integration.

POSSIBLE COMMUNITY DEVELOPMENT RESPONSES

The problems marginalised groups face accessing services, overcoming isolation and becoming integrated in their communities and society raise questions as to how community development might respond and facilitate positive spaces for reducing isolation. Key debates in community development over recent decades have centred on the tensions between top-down and bottom-up practice, and between a focus on the assets or needs of communities (McKnight & Kretzmann, 2012).

Mainstream and statutory services have most often imposed a top-down response to a top-down assessment of needs that can increase stigmatisation and fail to adequately address needs of particular communities. Such top-down interventions are rightly criticised (IDeA, 2010). One example of this is the UK's Prevent duty which has been criticised for scrutinising Muslim communities disproportionately and framing them as dangerous (Abbas & Awan, 2015; Coppock & McGovern, 2014). The deficit-discourse that informs such interventions increases the stigma and marginalisation of particular groups. Former Prime Minister David Cameron, for example suggested that migrant Muslim women who don't integrate are vulnerable to extremism and he challenged them to learn English within 2.5 years of arrival in the United Kingdom or face deportation (Governance Now, 2016). The focus on top-down hard outcomes, such as language learning, as key identifiers of integration is problematised by Anjum, McVittie, and McKinlay (2018). This suggests that while language learning may be a key support issue, it is also being used as a key punitive argument in relation to integration, despite a lack of sufficient funding for ESOL classes (Refugee Action, 2017a). It also reflects the problems with top-down policy measuring outcomes in only narrow ways, as identified in the previous chapter where paid employment is the key integration impact measure used in relation to attendance at ESOL classes (Cooke & Simpson, 2009; Klenk, 2017).

In the climate of austerity, localism and of shrinking the state, Featherstone et al. (2012) have introduced the concept of 'progressive localism' as an alternative. Featherstone et al. are deeply critical of 'austerity localism' and frame it as the latest implementation of a form of politically driven neoliberalism that imposes market values on public services in order to justify the reduction of welfare provision. Progressive localism is not a politically compliant collusion with neoliberalism but involves active resistance to it. For organisations committed to social justice, there is a need to challenge the division and inequality created by right-wing discourses that ignore structural factors and promote self-help, austerity and fear of others. A two-way integration approach (as explored earlier) would allow for practice that both supports individuals whilst recognising structural challenges that need to be addressed to support the integration of marginalised migrant groups.

Asset-based community development (ABCD) has been championed in community development over recent decades as the solution to problematic practice and policy-making (McKnight & Kretzmann, 2012). ABCD is based on the premise that by focusing on 'capacity, skills, knowledge, connections and potential in a community', practitioners and services are able to see beyond 'problems that need fixing' whereas a focus on deficits

> ...designs services to fill the gaps and fix the problems... As a result, a community can feel disempowered and dependent; people can become passive recipients of services rather than active agents in their own and their families' lives.
>
> (McKnight & Kretzmann, 2012, p. 7)

ABCD removes the power dynamic of institutions and services defining people by their problems and, instead, enables them to be empowered in shaping their own solutions and services.

However, whilst ABCD has a clear role to play in reducing top-down stigmatising of communities, it has been argued it may overlook or even cement inequalities (MacLeod & Emejulu, 2014; Missingham, 2017). The focus on assets over needs may mean needs of marginalised groups are ignored. As such, MacLeod and Emejulu (2014) critique ABCD as colluding with neoliberalism; justifying privatisation, individualism and austerity. For example, in the recent UK political context, which has centred on localism and on rolling back the state, we have seen significant cuts to statutory funding for ESOL classes and yet, as already outlined, a lack of English language proficiency has been clearly identified by Government-commissioned research as a key isolating factor for marginalised migrant groups (Change Institute, 2009; Refugee Action, 2017a). There is therefore an argument for an explicit focus on needs (in order that these aren't disregarded) and on tackling these in positive ways in work with the most marginalised and excluded communities.

This is not to argue against asset-based work with groups that have developed the social and knowledge capital to utilise this approach; there are many positive examples of this. In Canadian research, Eidoo (2016) found that young Muslim women were developing their own community-based and after-school spaces in which they took refuge from Islamophobia and racism, as well as from cultural patriarchal restrictions, and were developing their own forms of learning, community and citizenship. However, this relies on the women having a certain level of social and knowledge capital and resources, and may not work for new migrants or those most marginalised. Marginalised groups need local services that resist neoliberal ideas of 'self-help'

(Berner & Phillips, 2005; MacLeod & Emejulu, 2014; Missingham, 2017). This means not solely viewing people through a lens of deficit, as well as not disregarding their needs and recognising how these are compounded by structures and institutions, in order to be able to frame services around their unique challenges and their strengths to overcome them.

Some researchers have argued for more balanced models. Missingham (2017) argues that if ABCD is brought together with a critical pedagogy in community development then the problematic collusion with neoliberal discourse can be avoided. Nel (2018) compared the use of needs-based and asset-based approaches with community groups in South Africa. She found that needs-based approaches had a greater effectiveness in the short-term whereas ABCD had greater sustainability. Based on research with Mexican immigrants in the United States, Hebert-Beirne et al. (2018) argue for a community-driven (bottom-up) approach that identifies and responds to both needs and assets.

Mayo (2017) recognises that a neoliberal focus on meritocratic ideals and individual agency has led to a context in which those who need welfare and support are seen as at fault, disregarding broader structural inequalities. She gives the example of the housing crisis being blamed on migrants in populist and media discourse, rather than on governments that have reduced social housing stock and rich landlords profiteering from the crisis. This focus on those in need as in deficit and at fault has led to greater surveillance and control of such groups by government (Mayo, 2017), as seen in counter-terrorism policies that disproportionately target Muslim communities and in the detention of asylum seekers. Mayo (2017) recognises that in this context, broadening inequalities have been particularly exacerbated for minority groups. Paradoxically, it is arguable that a sole focus on assets may support such neoliberal notions of people's agency and resilience to overcome their circumstances, and actually allow deficit perspectives and individual blame to be reinforced where individuals or groups cannot overcome structural barriers.

As such, Mayo (2021) recognises that community development initiatives framed around self-help and resilience can reflect a neoliberal discourse that ignores broader social inequalities. She advocates for community-based learning initiatives, while emphasising that she is not 'in any way implying that deep-rooted inequalities can be resolved by communities on their own, without wider structural changes' (p. 111). She goes on to state that such forms of community-based learning should not be focused on 'promoting "resilience" as a backward-looking strategy for communities to turn inwards, as they attempt to pull themselves up by the bootstraps – rather the reverse' (Mayo, 2021, p. 111). This builds on other critiques of the use of the concept of 'resilience' as a neoliberal tool for disregarding structural inequalities (Ní Charraighe, 2019). It also supports our arguments for both a two-way integration process, and a balanced model of community development that incorporates a recognition of needs and challenges as well as strengths, assets and potential.

In the case of migrants and refugees in the United Kingdom, they may lack information or resources rather than skills or capacity. Therefore, increasing their social and knowledge capital (through teaching English for example) may be a route to being less dependent and more empowered. For grassroots, progressive community work this needs to involve a bottom-up rather than top-down assessment of needs and to resist the fear and division created by top-down deficit-focused interventions (Featherstone et al., 2012; Missingham, 2017). A needs-sensitive, bottom-up model may be effective in facilitating integration, not in top-down politically charged notions of integration, but a more holistic approach focused on the direct needs, assets and well-being of the community. Bottom-up interventions remove the power dynamic of top-down responses for a relatively powerless group, and allow for a needs-sensitive approach shaped around their particular intersections and challenges.

CONCLUSION

On first glance, it could be argued the women's project represents the form of practice championed by the UK Government since 2010 under 'Big Society' and localism agendas. However, cuts to funding for community services under the austerity era and flawed notions of localism, which justify state cuts whilst doing little to support grassroots initiatives, mean that small projects such as the women's project have decreased in recent years creating a dearth of bottom-up interventions (Mulvey, 2009; Refugee Action, 2017a). Where they do exist, they are subject to a precarious funding environment.

The literature explored in this chapter raises questions about whether policy and practice should focus on assets or needs, be top-down or bottom-up, and how services can overcome the challenges that compound rather than reduce the isolation of migrant communities. The literature highlights the need for more accessible services for refugee and migrant women. The proceeding Chapters (5, 6 and 7) will outline how these debates are responded to in our research, through the qualitative data and, in particular, how the women's project worked towards reducing isolation, creating accessible bottom-up services, responding to needs as well as building on assets over a three-year period.

These chapters will demonstrate the opportunities and challenges that emerged from the particular model of practice adopted by the women's project. For example, through starting with a needs-based approach that provided English classes, topical workshops, social engagement and individual support to address the deficit of both social and knowledge capital before building on assets, for example through women-led workshops (see Chapter 6) and women becoming volunteers and staff (see Chapter 7). Particular challenges faced by the project centre on the precarity of funding, reliance on volunteers and disruptions to consistency often created by these precarities. This raises questions over how such services collude with or challenge neoliberalism and austerity.

5

FROM ISOLATION TO ASPIRATION[1]

This chapter presents the qualitative findings from the first year of the research. The key themes that emerged related to the women's happiness and wellbeing, confidence, knowledge and skills, integration, freedom, and empowerment. The chapter considers how change began to occur in the first year of the project through sustained engagement and positive relationships with project staff and volunteers. This change, however, was more aspirational than tangible, demonstrating the need for long-term support to facilitate more sustainable change in work with the most marginalised migrant and refugee women.

Alongside the funded women's project activities (which centred on the provision of monthly workshops and some one-to-one support), the charity was delivering a significant amount of work 'in kind'. This included weekly rather than monthly provision, ESOL classes before each weekly workshop, and on-site childcare provision. This weekly and holistic provision sustained the women's engagement with most women attending regularly. Throughout the first year, the women's project ran in both south-east London and west London.

In year one, the project appeared to be achieving its aim of engaging Muslim women from conservative families that other services fail to reach – and was working towards its aim to facilitate their empowerment and integration. The charity was working towards this aim through providing a women-only space weekly in which to deliver the project activities. The project

---

1 The qualitative findings presented in this chapter are an extended version of the year one findings also published in an article: Thompson, N. & Nasimi, R. (2020) 'This place means freedom to me': needs-based engagement with marginalized migrant Muslim women in London, *Community Development* Journal, 2020, doi:10.1093/cdj/bsaa029.

had recruited staff, volunteers and speakers the women attending could relate to and aspire to.

The women's project had not yet achieved its long-term aim of encouraging the women attending the project to volunteer to lead events and workshops. Women were volunteering to cook, bring and share food at the workshops. Women were developing solidarity and support for and with each other. They had not yet volunteered to lead workshops, though their participation, contribution and peer support in these contexts grew over the first year.

Another aim was to see impacts of the women's empowerment in their own lives and those of their children and families. In year one, women clearly expressed the desire and intention to make changes to their lives in workshop evaluations and interviews (for example, to learn to drive and to engage with their children's schools). These intentions were largely aspirational rather than concrete at the end of year one, reliant on further progress in learning English as well as confidence and knowledge to engage with schools and other systems.

The qualitative data presented in this chapter are drawn from workshop evaluations as well as 15 interviews with nine women's project participants, five volunteers and the project coordinator. Volunteer interpreters were present for the majority of interviews with project participants. All names used in interview quotations and case studies are pseudonyms.

WHO ATTENDED THE WOMEN'S PROJECT IN YEAR ONE?

In year one, 71 different women from a wide range of countries of origin attended the women's project, most of whom attended regularly. Attendance grew throughout the year. The project coordinator engaged in outreach outside local schools and the women themselves spread the word to friends and acquaintances in their communities. Eighty percent of women who engaged with the project in year one attended for two months or more, with 54% attending for five months or more. This repeat attendance was key to supporting the women's empowerment over time.

Forty-four percent of the women were from Afghanistan with the other 56% from 16 other countries of origin. They were aged between 25 and 49 years, and 81% had children. The background of the charity's founders (being from Afghanistan) and the relatability, language and critical mass of participants from Afghanistan this brings led to the large proportion of women from Afghanistan attending, whilst the project was also proactively reaching wider groups.

THE WORKSHOPS

The funding for the women's project was centred on the provision of workshops on issues relevant to the women's lives, and to reducing their isolation and facilitating their integration in their communities and society. These workshops were facilitated by female speakers, most with relatable ethnic backgrounds or experiences. Interpretation into Farsi and Pashto was provided at most workshops by volunteers. After workshops, the women were supported to complete a simple evaluation form that had been devised, trialled and amended in collaboration with volunteers and participants to ensure it was a useable document for women who speak a range of first languages. Only a small number opted out, usually when they needed to leave before it was completed (many relied on volunteers supporting them to complete it). Overall, across the workshop evaluations in year one of the project: 94% of attendees reported the workshops as relevant to their lives; 88% of attendees reported increased knowledge through the workshops; 93% of attendees reported they would do something differently in their lives as a result of the workshops.

In the first year of the women's project, the workshops focused on a range of topics such as life coaching and setting goals, challenging gender stereotypes, women's equality, CV writing, sharing migration journeys, health and wellbeing, relaxation techniques, parenting, education, dental care, and learning to drive. As such, there were workshops that focused on issues of empowerment as they relate to understanding issues of gender and inequality, as well as more practical workshops that focused on the specific information and knowledge needed by the women to set and make progress towards their goals.

Women directly requested topics for workshops with the 'learning to drive' workshop, for example, being in response to their request raised in evaluations and interviews. As such, although women were not yet delivering peer-led workshops in year one, they were actively contributing to shaping the topics for workshops.

Evaluations from the year one workshops demonstrated how the women were beginning to raise their aspirations, reduce their isolation and move towards empowerment. The workshops were an essential part of them building social and knowledge capital in order to begin to imagine such changes for their lives. For example, workshops on 'challenging gender stereotypes' and 'equality for women' raised the women's awareness of inequality whilst building solidarity between them. This is seen in comments recorded in the workshop evaluations such as:

> I'm going to believe in myself. Women should not be scared, they are not less than men.

I want all girls to study, like how they can study here, we need to help the young generation.

I want to learn more so I can help others like myself.

It reminded me of women's strength. I enjoyed learning from each other, listening to each other's stories.

This combined with the more practical workshops on issues like the education system and learning to drive meant that these broad aspirations for women's equality could become more focused into specific aims for their own and their children's lives. Examples of these developing aims were recorded in the workshops evaluations as follows:

I learned more about the college system for my daughter.

I know how to help my children now, I will help them with their homework.

I learned about the different subjects in secondary schools – I realised the school has a lot of options.

I was scared before but now I want to learn how to drive.

I now really want to learn how to drive. My husband does all the driving. I want to be able to do it as well.

These examples demonstrate that while many of the women's starting points were from a point of isolation, they were learning about the inequalities and divisions that exist, and expressing a desire to overcome them. For many of them, attending a women-only space was essential to being able to attend, but through their engagement they were building aspirations to break down such gender divides in their own and/or their children's lives.

QUALITATIVE THEMES FROM THE YEAR ONE DATA

The women's developing aspirations occurred over time rather than as a result of attending a single workshop or event. Engagement over time allowed for solidarity and social capital to develop as well as for knowledge capital to build over time. In the interviews, the women were asked what had been significant about the women's project for them and what difference, if any, it had made to their lives. In year one, the changes articulated by the women were more aspirational than tangible, and represent the development of knowledge and social capital that led to them building new connections, increasing their confidence, gaining a greater sense of wellbeing, and developing the desire to change aspects of their lives.

Happiness and Wellbeing

The interviews with women's project participants were overwhelmingly positive with the women reporting feeling happy and excited simply to be at the women's project and among the other women.

> *When I come here, I get happier, meet new people.*
>
> *(Fawzia)*

> *The social time is the favourite bit for me. I've made new friends, made new connections.*
>
> *(Laily)*

These comments demonstrate how reduced isolation leads to an increased sense of happiness and wellbeing.

Having a space focused entirely on their own needs was also a new experience for many women. Some of the workshops focused specifically on health and wellbeing, including relaxation and stress relief. Comments on the evaluations of the relaxation workshop illustrate the women beginning to think about their own wellbeing:

> *I learnt how to take deep breaths to calm me down when I am stressed.*

> *The session calmed me down. I will focus more on what makes me happy.*

For these women, it was the first time they had stopped to think about themselves and what they need to relax and be healthy. Most of the women interviewed reported that attending the women's project was the only time they take for themselves to focus on their own health, wellbeing and happiness. This emerged both when reflecting on specific workshops focused on wellbeing issues, as well as when considering the project more widely.

> *One of the classes was about healthy eating and fitness. I had heart surgery last year and I learned about healthy eating. I also benefited from techniques like how to relax, how to know when I'm tired... I've sometimes felt depressed because of my illness as well but when*

I'm here I forget all the pain and I'm happy. I don't even know how the day is passing so quickly when I'm here. All I've done for six years is walk to the nursery and school and back but now there is something different.

(Mariam)

Mariam's experience illustrates how for some marginalised women, they can be in the United Kingdom for several years without any opportunity to reduce their isolation. The women particularly reported not having much opportunity to take time for themselves because of caring responsibilities. Childcare was provided by volunteers at the women's project where children could get help with their homework and/or attend classes to learn their parents' native languages. The women reported this was key to them being able to attend. While justifying time for themselves was not always easy, the women's project had become a space for focusing on their own wellbeing.

Confidence

All interviewees reported feeling more confident about their lives in England since attending the project. Whilst the women could identify things they still needed to learn, this demonstrated their perception of themselves as more able to live and function independently in British society. This growth in confidence was reflected in the women articulating longer-term goals around accessing services, obtaining a driving license, getting a job or supporting their children's education. The volunteers interviewed all expressed the importance of the women growing in confidence and how this supported their empowerment.

The biggest impact on the women is confidence, their ability to make some friends and improve their self-esteem. For example, some of the women that come are very quiet in the beginning but later on they start to talk about life... and also the way they dress and how they appear changes.

(Lucy, volunteer)

This growth in confidence was seen as a crucial starting point for the women achieving wider changes in their lives, reducing their isolation and building their courage to engage with people and other agencies.

Knowledge and Skills

The women's project provided the women with new knowledge and skills. In workshop evaluations, 88% of women reported an increase in knowledge. In workshop evaluations and interviews, women stated they would use their new knowledge in positive ways; for example, to implement techniques learned around relaxation, be able to access healthcare and other services without help, or feel better prepared for their driving theory test.

In interview, Mursaal explained how she had learned about her local area and how to use computers for the first time through the methods used in the workshops.

> *I have learned about housing and my area. I have learnt about computers, it's really good! I like learning more about computers.*
>
> *(Mursaal)*

She recognised how using computer programmes in the workshops to write a CV and prepare for a driving theory-test had led to her becoming more computer-proficient.

The women also identified the English classes as being significant to them feeling more empowered in their lives. Women who had been in the United Kingdom for several years without learning to speak English reflected particularly on the impact of the project's ESOL classes.

> *I started from zero. I felt blind and dumb, not able to speak. I felt so depressed because I was feeling if I see someone in the street, what will I say? I was scared of communication.*
>
> *(Razia)*

> *It's amazing because I now have the basic sentences I need in everyday life, like booking appointments. This is an amazing class... I travel over an hour on the bus even if I'm ill.*
>
> *(Mariam)*

It was apparent from the women's narratives that learning English increased their sense of independence and longer-term goals for their lives. It coincided with knowledge gained in workshops on issues such as health and schooling to enable them to articulate and work towards these goals. The women felt that they needed to achieve these goals in order to gain a greater sense of dignity and independence, describing humiliating past experiences.

> *I want to go shopping without being scared. I want to go to the doctor without someone else there. I have the coil – I couldn't tell my daughter because I'm embarrassed. I had an interpreter. I dream of the day I can talk to the doctor without telling someone else. I wasn't sure the interpreter got it right. My husband doesn't have to take me shopping any more. It's simple stuff. When I want to buy onion or garlic, I know how. I live here and I didn't know basics. Once I wanted to buy spinach. I went into the shop three times, I had to go home and get the empty bag. And now I'm learning… I always ask my husband to go to parents' evening at school and I'd like to go myself. When I can read school letters, I can better prepare my children, like when they need to wear a special costume.*
>
> *(Nargis)*

Learning English was identified by the women as key to fulfilling long-term goals for independence whilst engaging with the workshops was instrumental in them identifying the goals and skills they wanted to aim for. For example, one of the women stated: 'When I can speak English better, I would like to volunteer and help other people. That is a goal for me'. Another said: 'I need to improve my English so I can get a job'. This demonstrated that they desired to both support themselves and others around them, through the knowledge and social capital gained through their engagement with the project.

Moving from Isolation towards Integration

A key aim of the women's project was to support the women's integration, and this was happening at a range of levels, from with each other, to beyond the project and in wider society. Many of the women did not have friends they socialise with outside their family so the opportunity to meet other women was a significant change for them.

> *I am from Iran and I have met people from Algeria, Iraq, and Afghanistan. I like seeing my friends.*
>
> *(Mina)*

> *We take turns to bring food and I really enjoy bringing food and sharing with others. I wait the whole week to see these women, they are like sisters.*
>
> *(Nargis)*

Beyond this social integration, the development of confidence, knowledge and skills supported their wider integration, as well as the moral support of having a friendship network beyond their family.

The women explained how the project's staff and volunteers supported them with their integration and access to services beyond the project.

> *The staff have given me help with the citizenship test. They are very good, they help us… What you need, you can find here. If they don't have the information you need, they tell you where to go. For example, I needed a solicitor and they helped me find where I could get help.*
>
> *(Fawzia)*

This demonstrates the importance of having a range of long-term support in one community organisation where the staff understand the communities they are serving and have built positive relationships with them. It also illustrates the two-way model of integration outlined in Chapters 1 and 4 where the women were supported by those around them in a culturally accessible space, but encouraged to engage further with their communities and society. Through this support, the women were building the knowledge capital and social support necessary for their independence and empowerment goals.

Freedom and Empowerment

For many of the women, accessing the women's project brought freedom from barriers that limit their full integration in their communities and society. These barriers included, among others: not knowing English; not having information about their rights, health, or where to get help and support; and not understanding the school systems their children were going through. These reflect the barriers identified in the Casey report (2016) and outlined in Chapter 4. Their narratives in the sections above show how increased knowledge, confidence and skills in these areas helped them to move towards empowerment.

In addition to this, many of the women were isolated by the expectations of their families and culture about what is appropriate. The project coordinator, Aleah, described a process whereby many women 'bring their four walls of isolation with them' when they come to the United Kingdom because they don't leave the house other than for chores and don't socialise beyond their families. Arguably, this isolation is further entrenched by prejudice towards Muslim and migrant groups. Some of the women explained how they couldn't go anywhere else because their husbands wouldn't let them or because of childcare responsibilities.

> *The best thing is I can't go anywhere else to study because I have two children and I can bring them here and they are well looked after. I don't get that support anywhere else.*
>
> (Laily)

> *This place means freedom to me because my husband didn't let me go to college, but I explained there are no men here.*
>
> (Mariam)

The sense of freedom described by Mariam is a powerful articulation of the impact of receiving holistic and culturally accessible support.

All the above themes came together to support the women's empowerment. This ranges from the simple yet powerful examples of women going to the doctor, dentist or shops alone for the first time to those working towards ambitions such as finding work or learning to drive. Many of the examples of empowerment were facilitated through a combination of social integration, learning English and gaining new knowledge through workshops. The volunteers also recognised the importance of their work in empowering the women through them gaining both social solidarity with each other and the information and resources they needed to expand their view of their own futures and capabilities.

> *They have more information about what services to access, they have the skills to be able to ask for the resources. There's the resources of the staff here, we're able to guide them, and there's the resources they have in each other... The fact they can go to one another and get advice and learn how people have done it... But as well as that we've been teaching them things like going to the doctor's and about the British school system, a presentation that teachers came and did, that really supported them to know how the system works, that their children should be getting homework and to know what's expected of their children so they can support them in the best way and ask for help at school. So, it's really about empowering them with understanding how systems work and where to go for information.*
>
> (Anousheh, volunteer)

This social and knowledge capital was something the women weren't acquiring anywhere else.

For one of the older women (Nargis), for example, who had been living in the United Kingdom for a long time but had never been shopping without her husband, having the knowledge and confidence to do so was a simple yet powerful change. For some of the younger women, their ultimate goal was to find a job. For many of the women, the liberations they aimed for were for their children. For example, wanting them to have educational opportunities they did not have themselves. The aims for their own and their children's empowerment were informed by increased knowledge about inequalities women face combined with practical knowledge about UK systems, as seen in the examples shared earlier where women aspired to learn to drive or to support their children's study. The development of solidarity with each other as well as gaining such information supports the development of their social and knowledge capital.

For some of the women, their starting point was one of almost complete isolation, as in the case of Mariam. Therefore, hard outcomes favoured by policy such as gaining employment or achieving English language qualifications are not possible to facilitate through short-term engagement. However, the value of the women's engagement is not absent if they have not gained employment or met hard, measurable outcomes. This is seen in the qualitative findings presented from the women's interviews where simple changes made a big difference to their sense of wellbeing or even freedom. It is also captured in the case studies of particular women that staff and volunteers shared with the academic researcher. An example of such is below, illustrating how the project's holistic model of provision led to reduced isolation and developing aspirations for the most isolated women, and the impact of this on their wellbeing.

Case Study: Nasrin

Nasrin came to the United Kingdom a few years ago as an asylum seeker having fled the Taliban insurgency in Afghanistan. She has refugee status. Shortly after she arrived in London, her husband abandoned her. Nasrin found out about the charity through a stranger she met after becoming upset whilst shopping. She recalls that the woman drove her home and promised to return. She came back with the contact details of the charity after searching the internet for local community organisations.

Nasrin was invited to join the women's project. She has participated in workshops on topics such as rights, issues relating to children and families, and health. Nasrin also attends English classes and gets assistance from the legal advocacy group. She has become an active participant in the charity's women's sports classes, taking part in activities such as yoga. She cannot afford gym membership and the sports classes help with her mental and physical health, especially as she suffers from diagnosed depression.

(Continued)

Nasrin described the project as 'family' stressing that 'life without friends and family can be a lonely and depressing place'. She has met new friends and she said that, along with the social connection, it gives her a sense of purpose and identity. Nasrin was lacking self-confidence but now realises women can support themselves, make decisions and control their own lives. She said that her understanding of gender relationships has changed since she started coming to the project; she now thinks relationships are a team where both work together rather than one being in charge of the other.

Taking part in English classes and workshops has helped Nasrin to imagine new possibilities. She said she would like to learn to drive and work for a charity like this one to help other women realise their potential. She described the project as having given her a voice and a sense of identity as a woman. 'They have made me feel human', she says.

CHALLENGES

There were some challenges that emerged in the year one data. These largely stem from the precariousness of a small project relying on volunteers and limited funding. The full model of provision was only possible through the work of staff and volunteers beyond the funded hours of the project. Much of the work was delivered 'in kind' and subject, at times, to change and disruption. The women were reluctant to offer criticism of the project in interviews and expressed discomfort when asked what could be different. A couple of the women approached the academic researcher after their interviews to raise some issues for improvement around the consistency of ESOL teachers and childcare. One of the women did raise these issues in the interview itself. Laily stated that 'one thing we have struggled with is the English teacher has changed a lot', reflecting on the need for 'stability' in the relationships the women develop with staff.

Laily also stated that 'one of the reasons I come is for me and the kids get looked after which is good but it is a long day for them'. Reflecting on the fact that friends she had invited were unable to attend because 'not all husbands are willing', she said that if children had 'more structured lessons' or were 'learning about the Quran or culture' it would help persuade husbands. This reflects a clear challenge in engaging the most isolated women. However, the women's project was reaching women who did not engage with other services and was able to build trust with some husbands because of its foundations within the communities it served.

The changes the women articulated for their lives were more aspirational than concrete in year one. This development of aspirations is arguably an early stage of the empowerment process. The fact that the women's empowerment was largely not yet tangible or sustainable arguably demonstrates the importance of long-term support for marginalised migrant women.

CONCLUSIONS

In year one of the women's project, it appeared that the project provided a safe and informal space in which women could access individual support, social integration, English lessons, childcare, and workshops relevant to their lives. The women's narratives drew on the importance of their developing social solidarity, as well as the learning gained from workshops and English classes. Each of these elements contributed to the women's developing empowerment, which occurred over time rather than as the result of attending a single event. In year one, their empowerment was largely aspirational, with the women beginning to talk about how they would like things to be and to set goals for their lives. Tangible changes to their lives beyond the soft impacts of being more connected with each other, and having an increased sense of happiness and wellbeing, were not yet being manifested for a lot of the women.

For many of the women, the initial draw was the women-only English classes and it is from these that they went on to access workshops and other support. Whilst these English classes were often the focus for gaining skills, it is the workshops that provided the knowledge, confidence and social engagement that motivated the women to use these skills to set goals for their wider lives, such as attending the doctor without their husbands or children accompanying them, being able to communicate with their children's teachers, or looking for work or volunteering opportunities. In interviews with project participants, the women were beginning to articulate how their improved English skills and new practical knowledge might translate into positive changes in their wider lives such as these. The weekly provision was key to the development of supportive relationships. The social solidarity built through regular engagement was key to their reduced isolation, improved sense of wellbeing, and development of confidence and long-term goals for their lives.

A large part of the project's success in engaging a hard-to-reach group of women was because they were a grassroots organisation, where people with similar backgrounds to the women worked to build trust over time with a sensitivity to the particular needs of the target group, demonstrating a bottom-up (rather than top-down) needs-sensitive approach. The staff's understanding of the target group and provision of the women-only space allowed them to provide reassurance to husbands, many of whom also accessed the organisation's services. Some of the women had been unable to access other services because of lack of support from their husbands or families.

The women spoke of the approachability of the staff and volunteers. Mariam, who had been particularly isolated, explained how she became involved after the women's project coordinator engaged in outreach work with a group of mothers outside of her children's school.

> [Aleah] went to the school and spoke to the Mums outside. I loved that she spoke with me in Pashto!
>
> (Mariam)

Once engaged with the project, the women were able to become fully involved in workshops because of the provision of interpretation into the main languages of those accessing the project. This was unfunded and delivered by volunteers. Women were also encouraged to translate for each other, especially where they knew languages not spoken by volunteers, and this formed a key part of their own empowerment and contribution to the project.

The project engaged a diverse range of speakers and workshop facilitators, many of them with similar backgrounds to at least some of the women attending, including speakers who were refugees themselves. This also reflects the bottom-up approach to providing workshops on practical issues as well as those focused on inspirational stories from role models. These appear to have been effective in supporting the women to articulate and work towards their own empowerment goals, as demonstrated in workshop evaluations and interviews.

However, the need to build trust with husbands emphasises that there are boundaries to the empowerment and integration for some women because of the family and cultural resistance some marginalised women face (Ali, 2015; Casey, 2016). This links to the 'four walls of isolation' described by Aleah, the project coordinator, in interview. This isolation, as well as the broader gendered and intersectional prejudice towards Muslim and migrant women, demonstrates the need for targeted services in safe community spaces.

However, in the austerity climate, such interventions are shrinking rather than growing with Refugee Action (2017a) stating, for example, that statutory funding for ESOL classes in England was cut by 60% and more than £100 million between 2010 and 2016. Most funded ESOL classes that do exist take place in formal educational settings such as further education colleges with mixed gender classes. The women's project did not have any funding for the women-only English classes and were offering these 'in kind'. A reliance on volunteers and of work provided 'in kind' could be viewed as a collusion with political ideologies of austerity localism and of rolling back the state (MacLeod & Emejulu, 2014). The charity, however, also engaged in awareness raising activities through conferences and events at local, national and European levels to campaign for the support needed for migrant groups. Another way in which the project resisted neoliberal values such as individualism is through facilitating an empowerment based on interdependence rather than simply independence. The social aspect of the project involved the women supporting and helping each other with English and through bringing food to share. This demonstrates a social aspect to the two-way integration process and a focus on building community.

The fact that the women were engaging in a safe space outside of mainstream provision and wider society suggests that there are some limits to the integration facilitated. The Casey report (2016, p. 8) states that 'where communities live separately, with fewer interactions between people from different backgrounds, mistrust, anxiety and prejudice grow'. For some of these women, it was the first time they had socialised beyond their families, let alone their own community, and therefore the steps towards integration are necessarily small. The primary focus of the project on people from Afghanistan was a strength with boundaries. It was key to its success in engaging marginalised women but also limited the diversity of engagement.

This demonstrates how inclusion is often necessarily inter-related with exclusion for marginalised groups. This is reflected in research by Bright, Thompson, Hart, and Hayden (2018) who found that in faith-based youth and community work, there needs to be safe *exclusive* spaces provided to facilitate *inclusion* for minority groups. It is also supported by Giusta and Kambhampati's (2006) research which found that engaging with a familiar community was key to feeling settled in the United Kingdom for female migrants from Asia and Africa. The fact that the women were engaged in groups where those around them have similar backgrounds, needs, and skills and confidence levels, means they were not intimidated. Similarly, issues around female health and equality could be discussed in a safe setting for the women because the other participants, staff and volunteers understood the cultural sensitivities. The need to provide tailored services for such groups of women is supported by Ali (2015).

The findings from year one of the case study show that the project was successful in reducing many of the isolating factors found in the literature, particularly social isolation and lack of English language (Casey, 2016; Change Institute, 2009). The increase in wellbeing for the women demonstrates a response was emerging to the high levels of mental health issues identified among marginalised migrant Muslim women (Social Policy Research Centre, 2014). Whilst the project is supporting positive integration this is not the politically-charged deficit-focused notion of integration promoted by top-down policy but a more mutual and culturally-sensitive process that necessarily takes time and does not lead to immediate hard outcomes.

The project staff recognised that the women had strengths, capacity and skills but that there was a clear need for knowledge and resources to facilitate their empowerment. Learning English, understanding UK education systems, their rights, health and a focus on their own wellbeing all contributed to a model of provision that responded to their needs. This model was needs-focused rather than starting with assets, but it was a bottom-up needs-based approach. In the second and third year of the project (see Chapters 6 and 7) there was a shift from needs to assets as the women increased their knowledge capital, and began to lead workshops and take on volunteering roles. This reflects other research, explored in Chapter 4, which found that a combined focus on needs and assets can be helpful, with needs-focused approaches having more short-term benefit and asset-based approaches more long-term sustainability (Hebert-Beirne et al., 2018; Nel, 2018).

Overall, the women's empowerment in year one of the women's project was aspirational rather than tangible or sustainable. The proceeding chapters will demonstrate how this developed over time, building a model of long-term empowerment that moves through these stages of aspirational, tangible and sustainable empowerment. In year one, increased social support, knowledge and confidence led to the development of aims and aspirations for long-term change.

6

FROM ASPIRATION TOWARDS INTEGRATION

This chapter presents research findings from the second year of delivery of the women's project. The women's project activities in year two were centred again on the weekly provision of workshops, with ESOL classes and childcare provided 'in kind' alongside. There was also a structured mentoring programme delivered by volunteers in year two that focused on working with the women to set goals and identify objectives towards these goals, with progress reviewed together in mentoring sessions.

In year one, the project was achieving its aim of engaging migrant Muslim women from conservative families that other services fail to reach, and was working towards its aims to facilitate their empowerment and integration. In year two, the project was achieving its longer-term aim of encouraging women to volunteer at events and workshops. Women were volunteering to cook, bring and share food at the workshops and to organise social events. Three of the women who attended the project also delivered workshops in year two.

Another aim of the project was to see impacts of the women's empowerment in their own lives and those of their children and families. In year one, women clearly expressed the desire and intention to make changes to their lives (for example, to engage with their children's schools and to see their children have opportunities for work and study they didn't have for themselves). In year two, some of these aspirations articulated in year one were becoming manifested in the women's lives.

In year two, several women were involved in an action-planning exercise with mentoring support. Through the paperwork completed as part of this action planning process, women demonstrated that they were achieving objectives towards their long-term goals. These goals included: to learn English; to engage with their children's education; to access services independently. Objectives they achieved towards these goals included: attending English classes and setting targets for their learning; helping their children with school work and attending school meetings; making and attending appointments; travelling on public transport; studying for their driving theory test. The qualitative themes that emerge from the women's interview narratives in year two reflect the women feeling safe and less isolated, building positive relationships, living healthy lives, learning English, accessing services, and engaging with their children's education.

In year two, the women's project gathered research data through a number of methods including registration forms, workshop evaluations, action plans completed with mentors, interviews with seven women, and reflections and case studies from the project staff and volunteers. In year two, the interviews focused on women who had engaged with the women's project for at least six months, in order to explore their empowerment over time.

WHO ATTENDED THE WOMEN'S PROJECT IN YEAR TWO?

In the second year of delivery the women's project took place in west London. Despite the project no longer being able to maintain provision in two locations concurrently (due to this not being funded) and therefore the women in southeast London no longer having access to the project, attendance grew overall. 101 different women attended the women's project in year two (in comparison to 71 across two locations in year one), many of whom attended regularly. Twenty-seven of these women had also attended the women's project in west London in year one and 74 were new attendees in year two. The women were from 19 different countries of origin, aged between 23 and 48 years, and 90% of them had children.

In year two, 56% of women attended the women's project for two months or more. While this is repeat attendance from the majority, a greater proportion than in year one attended for less than two months. As the funding for the women's project centred on the workshops, the project's data on attendance related specifically to workshop attendance. As such, some of these women may have attended English classes or other activities for a longer period but opted out of workshops, and therefore they would not have been recorded as women's project attendees (for the purposes of monitoring requirements for the funder) despite being on attendance lists for other activities within the organisation.

There were some workshops on potentially sensitive issues in year two (such as domestic violence and female genital mutilation) and the qualitative data presented later in this chapter suggests that while some women appreciated the safe space to discuss these issues, others may have felt uncomfortable, particularly where they were concerned about what their husbands or families would think. This may have led to some women opting out of the workshops while continuing to access other services. Others may have disengaged entirely.

Therefore, whilst there were higher overall numbers of women who attended in year two than in year one, it appears that a similar number formed the core group of regular attendees (with over half of the 101 attendees in year two and four fifths of the 71 attendees in year one attending for two months or more). This may suggest that smaller groups may be more effective at sustaining engagement over time. The charity maintained weekly 'in kind' delivery of the women's project and this sustained the engagement of the core group of women who attended regularly.

THE WORKSHOPS

I really like all the workshops. I really appreciated the domestic violence one because I was a victim. The driving one was good. The one on health – I learned how much oil to use in cooking. Everyone could give their opinions in the workshops and we learned new things.

(Gulzar)

The women's project centred on the provision of workshops on issues relevant to the women's lives and to reducing their isolation and facilitating their integration in their communities and society. As in year one, the workshops in year two were facilitated by women from diverse backgrounds, many with ethnic backgrounds or experiences the women could relate to. Volunteers from similar backgrounds to the women also acted as interpreters in workshops.

In year two, workshops covered a range of topics, some similar to year one and some new. These included workshops on parenting skills, domestic violence, family, cooking healthily, learning to drive, hate crime, female genital mutilation (FGM), schools and education, healthy lifestyles, and expressing feelings through art. In addition, three of the women who attended the project delivered peer-led workshops on confidence and inner beauty, tailoring clothes, and cookery.

Overall, 99% of attendees reported the workshops as relevant to their lives; 95% reported increased knowledge through the workshops; 97% reported they would do something differently in their lives as a result of the workshops. This is an increase in workshop impacts from year one (see chapter five). However, the particularly high score for relevance is affected by the fact that this particular question was omitted from the evaluations of particular workshops (e.g. domestic violence and FGM) to avoid coercing the women into admitting traumatic experiences.

The peer-led workshops were rated particularly highly, possibly reflecting the women attending wanting to support their peer facilitators as well as them being inspired by seeing their peers present. Comments made in the workshop evaluations supported both these reasons.

> *My English is not so good so I feel shy. She was very good and strong – she helped me want to be strong.*
>
> *I'm happy to see my sister shine.*
>
> *I learned that if I give myself a chance, nothing is impossible. I want to succeed in learning English so I can stand on my feet.*
>
> *It was lovely to see the ladies speak – I also want to present.*
>
> *Both ladies inspired me with their skills. I wish I could do something. I want to discover the skills I have.*

One of the project volunteers also reflected on the impact of the peer-led workshop on confidence, delivered by Dilara who had been attending since the first year of the women's project.

> *She talked about what confidence looks like and encouraged the audience not to give up when pursuing something they want. She asked us if we could pursue what we want and the response of the room was everyone cheering 'yes, I can!' She said her presentation was inspired by her past experience and how she feels she's overcoming barriers since coming to [the women's project]. She said she hopes her presentation will inspire the women around her. She wants to continue improving her English so that one day, in the near future, she can go to university.*
>
> (Dana, Volunteer)

These workshops supported the confidence and empowerment of the women who led them and served to inspire other women to want to do the same.

As in year one, workshop evaluations demonstrated that the women were becoming more aware of inequalities in society. In year two, there was evidence that the women understood how oppression was linked to their intersectional identities. This emerged in relation to gender, religion and culture, for example, in the evaluations of the domestic violence and FGM workshops:

> *Why is the whole world hurting women?*

> *Women should be looked after and protected. We need to support one another. We should not be silent.*

> *I will make sure this never happens to my daughters. I will speak out about this more in my community.*

> *I got inspired by what she was saying and how this is bad for women. I will talk to my friends about this topic. I had no idea so many girls went through it.*

> *It affects so many girls across the world. It must be stopped. It makes me sad that so many of my sisters are being hurt. This is 'haram'. The culture needs to change.*

The workshop on hate crime supported the women to explore how their status as refugees and migrants led to some of their experiences of being othered and oppressed by wider society (see the theme of 'feeling safe' explored below). The more practical workshops and the mentoring process provided the women with information, resources and support to translate these understandings of their experiences and oppressions into more tangible goals for their lives, as demonstrated in the sections below.

SETTING GOALS AND ACHIEVING CHANGE

A bespoke action-planning process was developed by the academic researcher (in collaboration with project staff and volunteers) in year two of the women's project, to support the women to set and achieve goals and objectives, and measure their progress towards these objectives. The action-planning exercise was optional for women attending the women's project. Women who took part in the initial action-planning exercise were then invited to take part in three months of mentoring with a volunteer mentor to review their progress towards their goals. Availability of mentoring was based on the capacity of volunteers to offer it. Thirty-six women took part in the initial action-planning exercise. Sixteen women engaged with a mentor for three months, through which they assessed their progress towards their goals.

The women who took part had a range of long-term goals. Many of these were inspired by the workshops they had attended. Examples of some of their typical long-term goals were as follows: learn English; be more involved in their child's learning; access new places and services independently (e.g. GP, shops, public transport); lose weight/become healthier. The women each set a number of small objectives towards these long-term goals. These included such targets as: attend a specified number of ESOL classes; learn five new words each week for five weeks; learn to write and recite their address and other contact details; make contact with their child's school teacher; read one book per week with their child; sit with their child while they do their homework and discuss it with them; role-play a GP appointment with their mentor; make an appointment at the GP surgery; travel on public transport to a new place; download a driving theory app and try out a mock test; walk for one hour per day.

As objectives were achieved, the women set further objectives with their mentors towards their goals. Whilst the women were not expected to fully achieve their long-term goals within the three-month period, one woman did feel that she had fully achieved the goal she set herself of being able to help her daughter with her homework from school. She did this through a combination of weekly objectives that included developing her own English through reading regularly and learning new phrases/topics, and sitting with her daughter each time she did her homework until she began to understand it better. By the end of the three months she felt that she had fully accomplished the ability to actively help with her daughter's homework in a variety of subjects.

Not all of the women attended weekly throughout the three months and so, in some cases, meetings with mentors were sporadic. Of the 16 women who initially signed up to the three-month mentoring scheme: 15 achieved at least one objective; 14 achieved at least two objectives; 11 women achieved at least three objectives; four achieved at least four objectives; one achieved six objectives; one fully completed one of her goals. The initial three-month mentoring scheme took place shortly before both a premises move and the project coordinator leaving the project, as well as other changes to staff and volunteers. As such, the action-planning and mentoring process was disrupted and whilst new staff and volunteers did reestablish it in year three, not all paperwork was kept up to date. This, again, reflects the disruption and inconsistency that can occur because funding and staffing for supporting migrant and refugee women is precarious and not prioritised in policy. However, one-to-one support was part of the women's project throughout the three years, at times more informally and ad hoc than at others.

QUALITATIVE THEMES FROM THE YEAR TWO DATA

As well as through the action-planning process, the tangible (as well as the softer) changes the women achieved in their lives in year two emerged in interviews, reflections and case studies. The themes outlined below reflect the changes to the women's lives that emerged from the qualitative data including interviews with women's project participants, and from case studies and reflections submitted by staff and volunteers. These themes triangulate and add meaning to the changes reported through the action-planning reviews.

Feeling Safe

The women reported a general feeling of safety at the Women's project that was reflected in them feeling they had grown in courage or confidence through their involvement over time. This manifested in their confidence to engage with each other, to learn English, and to set goals for their lives – with some women even facilitating workshops for their peers. Many of the women had not perceived mainstream services to be a safe space they could access and they reported that, because the women's project was different from these more formal providers, they had built the confidence and courage to sustain their engagement and deepen their participation.

> *After coming here I have built courage and I feel more confident. Before coming here, I tried to go to college but I couldn't keep going. I find this more helpful.*
>
> *(Darya)*

> *I like coming here. I am more confident now. I feel comfortable here.*
>
> *(Sadeen)*

Feeling safe, comfortable and having the confidence to keep attending was significant to the women's lives and their integration with society because many of them were not accessing any services at all prior to attending the women's project. Many reflected how other more 'outsider' services had not been easy to access.

In year two, several of the workshops engaged with topics relating to safety and protection. This was done in a culturally sensitive way by facilitators with relatable cultural backgrounds, making the women's project a safe space in which to address these issues for some women. The workshops on hate crime, domestic violence and FGM are particular examples where difficult topics were facilitated in a way that enabled the women to engage in discussion.

Whilst the project coordinator, Aleah, reflected that some of the women did express discomfort discussing these topics, particularly domestic violence, other women expressed how glad they were to gain a greater knowledge of these issues. For example, Gulzar, who was a domestic violence survivor stated how she wished she had known more about the different forms of domestic abuse sooner.

> *There is a restrictive order placed on my husband. I really liked the domestic violence workshop. When they talked about forms of control, I realised if I had come here sooner I wouldn't have taken the abuse for so long. He didn't let me take part in activities and being outside the home. He stopped me having money and told me who I could talk to.*
>
> *(Gulzar)*

Soraya, who had experienced a hate incident in public that had made her afraid to leave her home, outlined the impact the hate crime workshop had on her feeling safe enough to go out again.

> *One day I was walking with three friends and a man spat on us and told us to go home and that we were all immigrants. I didn't do anything because I thought the police would want evidence. But now I know what to do. Someone came from the Council and told us how to deal with situations like that and that I should go to the police. I didn't go out for a long time after it happened and I didn't want my daughter to see it but she was there. The workshop was so helpful to know how to deal with it. After the workshop I had more courage and wasn't scared anymore because I had the information about what to do and who to call. I felt confident leaving the house again, I felt like I knew I would be safe.*
>
> *(Soraya)*

This feeling of safety within and beyond the project was key to the women becoming more integrated and less isolated.

Reduced Isolation

A clear change to the women's lives through their engagement with the women's project was the social integration it provided them. As in year one, the women reported how making friends had been significant to their overall happiness and to feeling less isolated.

> *I have met people from Pakistan, Bangladesh, Somalia, people who are Arabic, from different countries. I can say 'hello' to them!.*
>
> *(Bahar)*

I have found Afghan friends and other friends from elsewhere. There's too many to name. I am very happy.

(Gulzar)

I feel really happy when I come here because I get to spend time with everyone. Happiness is coming here.

(Darya)

Some of the women had lived extremely isolated adult lives before attending the women's project, only leaving their home for necessary errands, and the socialisation and friendships they developed were a particularly significant change in their lives.

In terms of my life before here, I was always home. I was just a housewife. But now I have got involved in more things and I enjoy myself a lot.

(Soraya)

I feel happier since coming here. If we have any problems, we discuss them with each other. I have people to talk to… It makes me busy. In the past, I only stayed at home and took my children to school. I felt isolated, on my own.

(Gulzar)

This was also reflected in year one (see Chapter 5) when Mariam stated 'This place means freedom to me' because her husband had not let her attend anything else. For women who have experienced trauma in their lives, having a place to belong is also particularly significant. Gulzar, who was a domestic violence survivor and was bringing up her children without any family support, explained this feeling of belonging.

When I came here I felt like I found my home.

(Gulzar)

This also reflects the experiences of women in year one, where Nasrin (see case study in Chapter 5) stated that her engagement with people at the project gave her a sense of 'family' and enabled her to 'feel human'. The women also reported that they were meeting and communicating with each other outside of the project, and for many of them this was a new experience.

I have so many new friends from different places with different languages… I'm friends with everyone. I see some of them outside of here now.

(Razia)

The volunteers also recognised the significance of this social integration for the women and volunteers who attended the project regularly.

> *There are women from different backgrounds and with different first languages, so it's great they have the chance to collaborate and engage with one another. Over the weeks it has been really wonderful to get to know the women better and see their confidence grow... The other volunteers are also fantastic to work with, and from the first week I started I felt accepted and comfortable with everyone. There are people of all ages working together, from all over London (and the world!) with different experiences to bring to the sessions, creating a diverse educational environment for the women.*
>
> *(Mia, Volunteer)*

> *I learned about connecting to them as women, as people, building trust and establishing a relationship. I have learned about a part of my community that I didn't know much about before, and connected with others who I wouldn't ordinarily have the opportunity to meet and become friends with.*
>
> *(Sofia, Volunteer)*

The project was only successful in combating isolation and facilitating integration because its staff worked hard to ensure it was as accessible as possible for the target group. The women expressed that factors such as it being women-only, being able to bring their children, and having people who speak their native language had facilitated their engagement where other services had not been accessible to them.

> *It's women-only and I can bring my children, it's different to other classes.*
>
> *(Sadeen)*

> *There's classes for the children at the same time. The time of the classes is good for me... It's made lots of change for me. I've found something to do. I've learned lots from the workshops. Because people speak our language, it's easy to express our concerns.*
>
> *(Gulzar)*

Such expressions of happiness were common to the women's discussions of their reduced isolation across years one and two, and demonstrates a clear link between their increased social solidarity and their overall well-being.

Building Positive Long-Term Relationships

The project facilitated the women's development of positive long-term relationships both with each other as well as with staff and volunteers. Whilst their relationships with each other were significant to their reduced isolation, their integration was also enhanced by their relationships with staff, volunteers and mentors. For the women who were not engaging with other services, the women's project was the first place in which they formed positive relationships with professionals and this sustained their engagement. The women commented in interviews on these relationships as a reason for their continued attendance.

> *It's good to make friends and my teacher is great. She explains things in a way I understand and that's why I keep coming.*
>
> *(Mina)*

The project coordinator described this relationship-based approach as purposeful, and core to the success of the project.

> *Many of the ladies we are working with come from backgrounds and households where they might not be entirely appreciated and, in some cases, lack the full scope of love they deserve… It is important that such a marginalised and, in many cases, forgotten group of ladies, are able to have their voices heard, and to feel appreciated, and this is precisely what both myself and the team have aimed to give to them. Through simple acts of kindness such as talking to them, taking a genuine interest in their lives… embracing them for all that they are, whilst supporting them into becoming the best versions of themselves. We are filling in the empty gaps, providing the love and support that may be lacking elsewhere and, most importantly, increasing their overall confidence. This comes from simple measures. For example, assuring them that we believe they can do better and improve themselves, no matter how small or big their improvements. We ultimately recognise that any development they make, is still progress and we acknowledge this and praise these ladies. Thus, allowing them to acknowledge this themselves, and to implement this self-praise in their own lives.*
>
> *(Aleah, project coordinator)*

Here, Aleah's comment reflects both how the project staff recognised the needs of the women and some of the particular challenges they faced, whilst also recognising their assets and potential. Aleah observed such relationships as essential to the other impacts such as the growth in self-confidence that leads to concrete change in the women's lives. She also believed this purposeful relationship-based approach to be important to engaging and sustaining volunteers with the project as, they too, are engaging voluntarily.

> *The success of the project is dependent on a strong team of volunteers. We now have the strongest team we have had by far. This includes translators, teachers and mentors for extra one-to-one support. This, I believe, is due to maintaining extremely positive but assertive relationships with all our volunteer members as a crucial part of this project. Appreciating their time and effort for coming in to support the women, whilst giving them clear direction on what they can do, to ensure the ladies are fully comfortable and are able to achieve long-term progress. These volunteers are needed to ensure the progress and smooth running of this project and thus need to be shown our appreciation. The women are not overly comfortable when there are frequent changes therefore it is crucial to maintain the long-term participation of our volunteers.*
>
> *(Aleah, project coordinator)*

These long-term relationships were important to the women's engagement as they felt most comfortable with consistency. Several women commented in interviews that they found it difficult when volunteers changed and they had to start building new relationships with new people.

> *When [Sofia, a long-term volunteer] left I was heartbroken.*
>
> *(Soraya)*

Many of the staff and volunteers had similar backgrounds to the women and this allowed the project to facilitate culturally sensitive relationships and services. The women commented on this in interviews as the reason why they were able to engage with the women's project where they hadn't with other services.

> *You understand our culture and the responsibilities we have to our children – thank you for letting me bring them! I love [Aleah]! I'm just so happy here!.*
>
> *(Razia)*

Razia had been in the UK for seven years before she found the women's project.

The women's project used these culturally sensitive relationships and services to engage a particularly hard-to-reach group of women who were largely not engaging with other professionals or services. They were able, for example, to engage in appropriate outreach through engaging the women outside local schools, where they could speak to them in their own language and build rapport before they attended the project. Their engagement with the project also supported their personal relationships. Razia, for example, when talking about the difference the project had made for her, stated:

> It's helped my relationship with my husband. Compared to before, he sees that I am different. It's made us stronger.
>
> *(Razia)*

This reflects that the women's wider families were less suspicious of their engagement with the project than they often were with mainstream services. It also demonstrates that, for some women, their husbands were supportive of their empowerment.

Living Healthy Lives

For the women who attended the project, having space to focus on themselves and their own health and well-being was rare. The workshops relating to health were evaluated highly by the women. In particular, they appreciated opportunities to get advice and information around diet and exercise and establishing healthy patterns for their lives. In evaluation forms and interviews, the healthy lifestyles workshop in particular was discussed as an enjoyable opportunity to have some health checks as well as to receive useful information about health-related issues that were directly relevant to the women's lives.

> I really enjoyed the health workshop – they checked my blood pressure and I learned about different fats.
>
> *(Razia)*

One woman commented it was the first time she had had her blood pressure checked or weighed herself. Reflecting on another workshop on cooking healthily, one woman explained how useful it was that the presenters understood the status of food in their culture, as well as how they tend to cook, and thus how to apply healthier routines to this.

The women also recognised how the project supported their mental health and well-being. During year two, the project secured additional funding for a series of art workshops with the women. In interviews, the women reflected on how these workshops had enabled them to spend time focussing on themselves and their mental well-being.

It's nice not to study and do the art. It's therapeutic – the art is speaking my emotions.

(Sadeen)

The art workshops made me feel relaxed and so much better about myself. All your tensions disappear when you focus on a piece of art work and it's like you go inside the art.

(Razia)

The project supported the women to set goals and objectives around eating healthily, becoming more active, and accessing health services – which affected both physical and mental health. Several objectives were achieved including losing weight (where needed for health reasons), implementing regular exercise into their routines, and making and attending GP appointments.

Learning English

The most common long-term goal that the women attending the project shared was the desire to learn to speak English. The project was able to provide ESOL classes pitched at the right level to be accessible to women whose level of English is below the entry levels for other classes.

My social worker told me about the [charity]. The college wouldn't accept me and I needed a free class.

(Gulzar)

Because I am illiterate and hadn't studied in Afghanistan, here I've had the help to understand about my child's study and what they learn in school.

(Darya)

Darya's experience was impacted by the combination of ESOL classes and workshops. The workshops further supported the women's motivation to learn English, particularly where they observed the peer-led workshops, which were presented by their peers in English. As seen in the examples earlier in this chapter, the women shared in the workshop evaluations the sense of inspiration this created.

The women explained in interview how the ESOL classes were supporting their wider integration as their English improved and they understood how to engage with systems such as their children's schools.

> *It's a really good feeling to be able to understand what people are saying. From the beginning to now, I understand more about many different things. I am not as dependent on my husband about my children's education. I have clear communication with my children's teachers.*
>
> *(Razia)*

> *I understand the information from school and nursery and can talk to the teachers.*
>
> *(Sadeen)*

Learning English, alongside the information provided in workshops, supported the women in accessing a range of other services as outlined in the next section. The project coordinator, Aleah, recognised a lack of English language as the main barrier facing the women and the accessible English classes as the reason that many attended the women's project, describing the classes as their 'pathway in' to the project.

Accessing Public and Private Services Independently

The women discussed in interviews how they had become able to access services they couldn't previously. Contacting and attending their GP surgery, going shopping alone, and using public transport were also some of the outcomes reported by the women in the action-planning process. Reflecting on her objectives achieved through the action planning and mentoring, one woman stated: 'For the first time I booked a doctor's appointment. I wasn't able to do it before'. Similarly, Gulzar explained that the classes 'helped me with seeing my social worker because there isn't always an interpreter' demonstrating some of the barriers presented by mainstream interventions.

Some of the women used role-playing with their mentors to rehearse such scenarios. The women discussed the difference their improved English, alongside these opportunities to role-play, had made.

> *It's helped me with finding my way around and getting the right buses... It's also helped when I go to the doctor's and filling out forms and things like that.*
>
> *(Soraya)*

> *I can go to the GP and we can understand each other. I wanted to go by myself and speak independently and now I'm really happy I can do that.*
>
> *(Razia)*

Workshops also supported the women to gain the knowledge and information to access services and become more independent. The workshops around health, education and learning to drive were key examples of this and 100% of the women attending these three workshops stated in their evaluation forms that they would do something different as a result of the workshops. The women also discussed how the workshops supported their increased independence in interview. Soraya reflected on the hate crime and driving workshops in particular.

> They've helped me a lot with learning to drive and how to deal with situations like talking to police.
>
> (Soraya)

The volunteers also recognised how the workshops supported the women's growing independence. Dana, for example, reflected how a woman had spoken to her a while after the workshop on learning to drive.

> One of the women told me about recently passing her driving theory test. She said that she had not passed the first three times and she wanted to give up. Her husband had also told her to give up and forget it, but she was motivated. She went in again to take her test and passed! She talked about how she had gained her persistence and not given up.
>
> (Dana, Volunteer)

The women's growing independence was also supported by workshops that made them more aware of women's rights and the need to break down inequalities. Some of them described the impact of this new knowledge, awareness and freedom in powerful ways. For example, Mina stated in interview 'My eyes have opened up – I am more aware about everything'.

Engaging with Their Children's Education

The workshops, action plans and mentoring supported several women to commit to engage more with their children's education, as well as providing them with the knowledge and resources they needed to do so. Following workshops on parenting and education, several women stated in evaluations they would become more involved with their children's schools. Such workshops also inspired the women to think about how educating themselves would also support their children's education.

How can I teach my children if I don't know myself? I need to help myself to help them.

Education is important. I need to help my children. If I learn and study, they will too.

My education affects my children's education; I need to try hard for them.

Now I understand how important it is that parents are educated so they can help and support their children.

This is a clear example of how specific goals were informed by the women's broader developing understandings of gender inequalities in particular, as reflected in the comments on other workshops outlined earlier in this chapter about the importance of changing things for women and girls.

Many of the women's action plans included objectives related to engaging with their children's study and schooling. In interview, Mina reflected on having achieved her goal of being able to regularly and actively help her daughter with her homework.

It's helping my daughter – we are communicating better and I can teach her what I have learned here. It's a nice feeling to be able to help my daughter with her homework.

(Mina)

Mina had been in the UK for five years, without learning English or gaining enough knowledge and confidence to engage with her child's education, prior to her engagement with the women's project.

The women also spoke about the impact of their engagement with the project on their children's lives, both through feeling more equipped to help their children themselves as well as through their children engaging with classes provided by the charity during women's project sessions.

I feel very strongly about education – it's very important to have... I have had the help here to understand about my child's study and what they learn in school... And it's helped me in terms of going to meetings at my child's school. Before I couldn't, now I can.

(Darya)

It's helped my children because while I am here they get tuition on Maths, English, Science, and the Afghani language – and they've had good results in school.

(Bahar)

In one of the interviews, Gulzar, who had left an abusive marriage and been referred to the charity by her social worker, reflected on what she had learnt about parenting, both through the workshops and, perhaps more significantly, through receiving support and feeling happier, safer and less isolated.

> *It's helped at my son's school. I can help my son more. I'm listening to him more and understanding. In the past, because I was very upset, I didn't consider his problems as much.*
>
> *(Gulzar)*

The other impacts of the project such as feeling safe and being less isolated combine in this example to demonstrate the wider change to Gulzar's family life.

DISCUSSION AND CONCLUSIONS

The data presented in this chapter demonstrate the women were moving from aspirational empowerment in year one to making more tangible changes to their lives in year two. This illustrates the importance of long-term engagement with the most isolated groups over short-term interventions. The changes to the women's lives in year two manifested in the women feeling safe, being less isolated, building positive relationships with each other and with staff and volunteers, implementing healthy changes to their lifestyles, making progress in learning English, accessing services independently, and engaging with their children's education. As in year one, the overall success of the project rested on the provision of an accessible and safe, culturally sensitive, women-only space in which to access support, social integration, English lessons, childcare and workshops relevant to the women's lives. Each of these elements contributed to the women's empowerment, which occurred over time rather than as the result of attending a single workshop, class or event.

In the second year of the women's project, concrete changes to the women's lives were supported through them setting long-term goals and identifying and achieving objectives towards these. Many of their more long-term goals were yet to be achieved but they were making substantial step-changes towards these. For example, getting a job or taking up a certain career was a long-term goal for some that required other goals to be achieved first, such as being fluent in English or undertaking certain courses as well as softer objectives such as increasing confidence and overcoming cultural or family restrictions.

The changes the women made in their lives, however small, were significant both for the women themselves and their wider families, as they reported that increases to their own well-being and skills also impacted on their families. For example, being able to help their children with homework or simply having overcome their own fear and isolation to be more actively focused on their family. This is seen in the examples outlined in the above sections. Overall, there was significant evidence in year two of the project that the women were becoming more integrated and less isolated through making friends, feeling safe, accessing services independently, and engaging with their children's education.

The women's project was both needs-sensitive and recognised that the women had strengths, capacity and skills, and a clear role in empowering themselves and each other. In the second year of the project, three women attending the project presented workshops to their peers in English. This not only empowered the women presenting, but inspired those who observed them. The evaluation forms for these workshops were unanimously positive, with other women expressing the desire and motivation to be also able to gain the confidence and reach the stage in their English learning where they could also lead workshops. This demonstrates the shift from needs to assets as the women increased their knowledge capital, challenging the power and knowl-edge deficit that marginalised the women. This approach reflects the call for combined asset-based and needs-based approaches, and for ABCD to remain critical of neoliberal ideas of self-help (Berner & Phillips, 2005; Hebert-Beirne et al., 2018; MacLeod & Emejulu, 2014).

The project did face some challenges in year two which, once more, centred on the challenges to sustain precariously funded provision. The decision was made to deliver the women's project in one area of London instead of two in its second year. It continued to offer weekly provision, with many classes and workshops delivered 'in kind' and on a volunteer basis. This precarity and the disruption it brings to provision impacts on consistency for the women who, again, reflected on the impact of changes to volunteers and staff. As in year one, some of the women raised again in interviews that the childcare could be better structured and organised, whilst also expressing that being able to bring children at all was often what enabled them to engage. The structure of the children's provision fluctuated throughout the year between organised classes and children simply sitting in the women's sessions with their mothers. This again reflects the precarity of relying almost entirely on volunteer capacity and availability.

While the action-planning process focused on women setting individual goals, there was also a need for the women to recognise and overcome wider challenges such as restrictive cultural expectations and prejudice in society.

The project recognised these broader challenges and how the women were affected by them, as reflected on by the charity's director below.

> *Our staff and volunteers have found that Muslim women are being held back by widespread Islamophobia, racism and discrimination. One woman visiting our office said her father had suggested changing her name to help get a job. Through our contact with these women we found a strong work ethic and high resilience among Muslim women who are working hard to overcome these barriers, to study English, and to become more integrated. The women have also raised concerns that girls are encouraged by their communities to focus on marriage and motherhood rather than gaining education or employment and this also holds them back. The young women we have spoken to who are working towards gaining employment have reported barriers such as stereotyping and low expectations. We have been able to support them where they have found that other service providers perpetuate these barriers. The women we engage have told us how they have been targets of bullying and harassment and how wearing a headscarf makes them a particular target for discrimination in public or when trying to access services or work. Overall, the women identify cultural barriers in their communities and discrimination in public, when trying to access services, education or the labour market as some of the principal obstacles that stand in their way. Muslim women face unique challenges to maintain their identity while seeking to succeed in a new society.*
>
> *(Charity director)*

The director's desire for the women to be able to both 'maintain their identity' and 'succeed in a new society' reflects the charity's commitment to a two-way integration process, as outlined in chapters one and four. The women's project was enabling the women to see and overcome some of these challenges and to understand where to seek support and information, as seen in the workshops on topics such as hate crime, domestic violence and FGM. Their increased awareness of such inequalities demonstrates they were being supported to recognise structural barriers to integration rather than it being framed as entirely an individual issue, as neoliberal policy tends to.

Feeling safe was a significant theme in year two of the women's project, which arguably was needed in order to support the women's broader empowerment. It was this sense of safety that enabled the women to go on to achieve some of their goals and objectives, and to become more empowered in their lives. The presence of insider-practitioners and researchers was significant to participants feeling safe. It was also significant to the women's feeling of safety that the community project itself was a grassroots community organisation, founded by a refugee family for other refugees and migrants. As such, the sense of safety was established through the use of insider-practitioners. 'Feeling safe' would not have emerged as a research theme without the presence of insider-researchers, nor would the personal examples shared in the research have been shared with a research team of complete outsiders. The willingness of the women to engage in research was arguably impacted by them feeling safe within the project more broadly. Had they not felt safe, they would have resisted sharing such personal experiences with the researchers.

Building on the women feeling safe, their reduced isolation also emerged as a key theme in year two of the project. However, it could be questioned whether there are limits to exposing marginalised groups only to insiders. A key aim of the charity's work with women was to facilitate their integration in community and society. This arguably requires some level of engagement with *outsiders*, external services or those who are not the same. We suggested in chapter five that there may be some limits to integration where marginalised groups access specialist services where everyone shares similar characteristics and experiences. Arguably, such engagement has potential to reinforce isolation rather than facilitate integration. However, Bright, Thompson, Hart, and Hayden (2018) found that safe spaces need to be created for 'inclusion within', particularly for groups that are isolated and excluded by society, in order to support their inclusion more broadly. This was reflected in years one and two of the women's project in them forming new friendships with those they could relate to as well as those who were different from them, as seen in some of their comments earlier in this chapter. The women reported particularly that they had made friends with women from other countries.

This reflects the argument we made in chapter two that insider and outsider status are not binary. For some of the women, through the women's project, they made friends with people from outside their own community for the first time. This allows for a process of staged integration – where the women were able to feel safe and share some characteristics with women from similar backgrounds before making further steps towards their integration. This was reflected in women reporting that over time they were able to engage more with their children's schools, feel more confident and independent in a range of public places, and even (in year three – see chapter seven) seek voluntary and paid employment roles.

A key step towards these outcomes was having a space to learn English and about UK services and systems that was accessible and culturally sensitive. The outcomes achieved by the women would arguably have not been achieved through external services that the women had previously struggled to access. As outlined in chapter four, several research studies and reports have identified the barriers marginalised migrant and refugee women face in accessing mainstream services (Change Institute, 2009; Giusta & Kambhampati, 2006; Social Policy Research Centre, 2014).

Overall, this chapter has demonstrated how the women's aspirations from the first year of the project were developing into more tangible changes to their lives in year two. The next chapter will present data from the third year of the project and demonstrate how these changes became more sustainable – for example, as the women began to take on more substantial volunteering and staff roles in the women's project. These stories of empowerment and change help to illustrate a model of long-term empowerment, where change moves from being aspirational to tangible to sustainable over time for marginalised groups.

7

STORIES OF EMPOWERMENT
AND CHANGE

This chapter relates to the third year of delivery of the women's project. The chapter focuses on stories of empowerment that emerged from the data, building on year one of the project where women were beginning to identify their aspirations, and year two where they were starting to make more tangible changes in their lives. The case studies presented in this chapter represent more sustainable stories of empowerment than in the previous years, demonstrating how empowerment is a long-term process for marginalised refugee and migrant women. In year one, women clearly expressed the desire and intention to make changes to their lives. In year two, some of these changes were becoming manifested. In year three, some women achieved significant changes in their lives, supported over time by the women's project. Some became volunteers or even staff for the charity and beyond. Some were engaging in college or university study. To achieve these and other changes to their lives, the women overcame barriers such as isolation, domestic violence, as well as a lack of English language and other skills and knowledge needed to be fully integrated.

This does not mean that every woman who achieved significant change was engaged with the project for the full three years. Women came and went, while core groups formed and changed over periods of time, as is the case in any community work involving voluntary participation. Many women only found the project in its third year and had yet to develop their aspirations and begin to make tangible changes to their lives. The women who achieved the most significant change in year three were those who had attended for a year or more. This was supported by the social solidarity they had built with each other, support from staff and volunteers (many of who were former attendees themselves) as well as the knowledge, skills and confidence gained through learning English and engaging with workshops. Learning English remained a fundamental catalyst for empowerment and integration alongside the informal and social support offered by the women's project.

In year three, the women's project gathered research data through a number of methods including: the women's registration forms; workshop evaluation forms; action planning forms; 15 interviews with six participants, four staff and five volunteers. The lines between the women who were project participants and those who were volunteers or staff were increasingly blurred in the third year of the project due to several women having taken on leadership roles. Hence, some of the women taking part in volunteer and staff interviews reflected on their experiences of being former participants of the project. These women viewed their new roles as a direct result of their engagement with the project over time. In year three, the interviews were primarily focused on women who had attended for at least a year, in order to explore the impact of long-term engagement with the women's project.

In this chapter, case studies have been drawn from interviews with the women, volunteers and staff to illustrate the sustainable levels of empowerment achieved by women who had been engaged over time. The women's stories demonstrate the grassroots nature of the project in that many of the women who engaged with the project went onto become volunteers or even staff. From these stories alongside the data gathered over the three years of the women's project, we develop a 'journey of change' model that illustrates how women moved through the project towards their greater integration in community and society.

WHO ATTENDED THE WOMEN'S PROJECT IN YEAR THREE?

In year three, the women's project took place in two different locations in west London. The women who took part were from 18 different countries of origin, aged between 17 and 62 years, and 41% had children. This was a lower proportion of women with children than in previous years and reflected a new younger cohort of women becoming engaged in year three.

There were 68 individual women registered to the women's project in its third year. This is a decrease in attendance from years one and two. The women's project was unable to provide the same level of 'in kind' support as in the previous two years and this impacted on the numbers attending in the third year of the project. In particular, they were no longer able to provide the weekly women-only English classes that had sustained the women's engagement in previous years – though mixed-gender English classes were available via the charity at other times of the week. This may have meant the project was no longer able to engage some of the most isolated women in English classes. For example, in year one, Mariam explained that she had been unable to attend college because her husband had only allowed her to attend the women-only classes (see Chapter 5). In interviews in year three, several women mourned the loss of the women-only English classes. Alongside this, key staff changes and a move in location in the first half of the year caused disruption to the project in year three.

The project coordinator changed in the first quarter of the third year meaning relationships built were disrupted – with consistent relationships having been found to be significant to engagement in the previous years (see Chapter 6). At the same time, there were some changes to the team of long-term volunteers who had been supporting the project. There was also a change of location in the first half of the year as the charity moved offices to premises large enough to hold classes and workshops on-site, rather than having to hire this elsewhere, and there was a gap in provision while the move took place. Alongside these changes, there was not capacity to run the regular weekly provision delivered by the charity 'in kind' in previous years. Workshops took place at least monthly, in line with the funding for the women's project, and were being established more frequently in the second half of the year. This, once again, demonstrates the precarious nature of this form of community work which is under-funded and subject to a lack of any clear policy commitment to provide such services for marginalised migrant and refugee women.

These disruptions meant that in year three, some attendees were lost while some new women also began to attend. Because there were no longer weekly English classes running before the workshops, fewer women with the lowest levels of English language skills were engaged. Some of the women who had engaged over the previous years of the project also had improved their English significantly. As such, the cohort in year three had higher levels of English literacy overall. In the second half of the year, a small core group developed who attended regularly. Some of these women were new to the project and some had attended the project since year one or two. Among the women who had attended longer term, several were able to achieve some significant and sustainable changes to their lives, that reflected them becoming more empowered and integrated over time.

THE WORKSHOPS

In year three, women's project workshops covered topics such as: volunteering; the driving theory test; mental health; body and mind; dance; the British education system; parenting services and skills; healthy cooking and eating; coping with stress. Ninety-eight percent of attendees reported the workshops as relevant to their lives; 94% reported increased knowledge through the workshops; 88% reported they would do something differently in their lives as a result of the workshops.

As in year two, some of the women delivered peer-led workshops in year three. These workshops were an opportunity to share their own experiences of empowerment within and beyond the project with their peers. Mursaal, who had learned to drive after she attended a workshop in a previous year of the project, spoke to the women about the driving theory test. Farahnoush, a medical doctor from Afghanistan, facilitated a discussion on mental health.

Several workshops in year three had a particular focus on the women's mental health – in order to address issues with confidence, stress and personal wellbeing identified by the women as barriers to their empowerment in previous years of the project. These workshops responded to the importance of getting support for mental health to support integration, particularly after traumatic experiences of displacement and migration. The women recognised this, as well as identifying practical things they could implement to support their mental health, in the evaluations of the peer-led mental health workshop as well as the workshop on coping with stress.

> A really good workshop for refugee women and those of us who have travelled to the UK. It really helped with mental health and knowing how to get support.

> We learned about the small steps we can take to feel better. I liked learning about 'grounding'. I will try this at home when I am feeling worried.

In addition, the body and mind workshops, facilitated by a dance and movement psychotherapist, which drew on art and movement-based therapeutic methods, enabled the women to take time to focus on themselves and think about their past experiences. The workshop evaluations suggested that for some women it was the first time they realised the importance of this.

> I didn't think about myself and my mind before.

> As a woman I need to think about myself as well as my family.

These workshops using art and movement were enjoyable for the women, as was the separate dance workshop. 'Fun' was not a priority for many of the women but evaluations of the dance workshop in particular highlighted the women trying something new and having fun.

Dance can be an amazing exercise. I will dance more!

It was a great experience, I had so much fun.

The evaluations and interviews throughout the three years suggest that enjoyment through music, art and movement was something missing from many of their lives. It was also a breaking down of cultural barriers for many of the women, something that would not be possible without long-term engagement. For example, some women shared that that there were cultural restrictions to women's dancing in their home countries or cultures.

The level of openness and engagement required for the workshops based on dance and movement would not be facilitated by one-off classes accessed in a formal or unfamiliar environment with unfamiliar people. The women's openness to having fun and breaking down cultural barriers through trying activities such as dance in year three demonstrates how they were becoming more empowered. Alongside this, practical workshops on topics such as volunteering and learning to drive supported the women to make practical steps towards their empowerment. The case studies presented below demonstrate the women's understanding of their experiences, barriers and traumas – as well as them drawing on their assets and potential to make substantial progress towards their integration.

STORIES OF EMPOWERMENT

While numbers of attendees were lower in year three of the women's project, the core group of women attending the project reached new levels of empowerment and independence. This empowerment occurred over time and was manifesting in sustainable changes to the women's lives. Opportunities to work for the charity as volunteers or staff were, in particular, key stepping stones towards other opportunities including further study or paid employment outside of the project.

Several women took part in the action planning process in year three with individual mentoring to set and review objectives towards their goals. While the paperwork was not consistently kept up-to-date, for 10 of the women it was reviewed on a few occasions. The long-term goals identified by these 10 women included: to learn English; improve physical and mental health; learn to drive; travel on public transport; go to college; help their children with school work; book GP appointments; go shopping alone. Objectives that they set and achieved towards these goals in the year included: attending English classes; making changes to diet, exercise and lifestyle; talking to neighbours; booking driving lessons; taking the driving theory and practical tests; travelling with their children; finding and signing up to courses they were interested in; reading books with their children; talking to teachers and attending school events; role-playing appointments and phone calls. All 10 women achieved at least one of their long-term goals including learning to drive, starting further study, and going places alone for the first time. Other women still received both one-to-one and group support. Some of these women also identified the impacts of this support in interviews, such as taking on volunteering roles or engaging in further study.

Case studies have been drawn from the interviews that illustrate some of the significant stories of empowerment experienced by the women attending the women's project in year three as well as the impacts on the lives of staff and volunteers.

Fatima – Rebuilding Confidence after Domestic Violence

I've been coming here for two years. We share our problems. We try to talk about what we are suffering and find solutions and know we are not alone in our problems. I suffered from domestic violence. My husband totally broke my confidence and now I am building my self-esteem with these women. I'm a single mum with no help. My children come here to learn Farsi; at the same time that I am here, they are in classes. Becoming a volunteer has helped my confidence. I assist the project coordinator and work once a week in the office doing admin work, as well as using my experience to help stand up for other women. Because the people here are from my community, I feel comfortable and I can get the experience I need. I am happier and I have a lot of hope for the future. I'm studying events and tourism at college as well as gaining experience here. I have a good platform for finding a good job in the future.

Mojdeh – From Refugee to Project Coordinator

I was a human rights activist in Afghanistan where I studied law. I supported women and children and successfully campaigned to change the law around marriage. Because of my work supporting women's rights I had to flee the Taliban. I fled to India in 2012 and came to the

United Kingdom in 2015, with no English language and without my husband and children – they arrived later. When I came to the charity, they saw my skills and experience and this year I became the women's project coordinator. Before I had this job, learning English was much harder. I volunteered in a charity shop for eight months before I got this job. I see some of the same problems for women here as in Afghanistan. Men control their money. They don't speak out about domestic violence. I've seen women come here very upset, very sad. They leave happy because they talk and learn. Some women have lived here over 20 years and don't speak any English – their husbands don't let them do anything. Their children become integrated and so do their husbands – the women are left behind. They need more information and a push to know they can change – we give them both. They can't drive, swim or use services – becoming integrated is hard. They don't think about their own needs. We give them space for their needs. The women look at those of us leading the workshops and think that they can change and do more too.

Habiba – I Was Scared and Alone, Now I'm Going to University!

I am from Syria and was a refugee in Lebanon before coming to the United Kingdom through the UN resettlement scheme two years ago. I've been coming to the women's project for over a year. I've got to know new people. I've been to celebrations and events. My first opportunity here was to learn English and now I can communicate with other people and learn about their culture. I want to start working so I want to speak English well and help other people. I'm trying hard and getting better. I have tried new things through the workshops. We have done exercises to get to know our bodies and how they connect to our minds. We have a lot of laughs. I feel confident to ask for help when I need it. I feel more confident to speak to my children's teachers. I'm more confident to help them with Maths and Science. I studied pharmacy back home and now my English is better I can help them. We had a workshop on becoming a volunteer and now I have applied for volunteering roles. When I become a better English speaker, I want to help others here. When I faced a problem, I used to be scared and find no solution. Now I come here. When I moved to London, I felt scared and alone but now I don't. I'm very happy because the staff here have helped me get a scholarship to study a course at university. They have helped and encouraged me and given me this opportunity. I feel a confidence here. I can speak without feeling scared. It's like coming home.

Aminah – Becoming a PhD Student and Award-winning Charity Worker

" I've been involved with the charity for over 10 years, since I was in secondary school. I have been a volunteer and now I am staff. Working here has enabled me to have a better understanding of the challenges that first generation adult refugees face – as opposed to my own experience of arriving in the United Kingdom very young, growing up and going through the school system here. It's made me interested in supporting women's rights and given me an understanding of the injustice and inequality that exists even in the United Kingdom. Working with the women's project over the last three years has enhanced my skills and experience. I've been told I would be a good leader because of my communication skills with new audiences and marginalised groups. I won a 'We are the City' Rising Star award for charity work and was shortlisted for the 'Women of the Future' awards. My work with women and their children and the understanding it has given me has led to me starting a PhD study exploring the experiences of second-generation migrants from Afghanistan in London.

Firouzeh – From Volunteer to Staff

" I came to London from Afghanistan 10 years ago and have been coming here for the last year and a half. I looked on the internet for organisations helping refugees and I found the charity. I've made so many friends and learned so many things. Everywhere I go, I say 'hello' to people who are from Afghanistan, or who are from Arab, or from other places. I was a teacher in Afghanistan so I became a volunteer for the women's project and I am a teaching assistant in the children's classes. Six months ago, I became a staff member. I can help people be better and change myself. I help organise the women's events now. I am not focusing just on my job, I help other people as well. I have learned more in the last year and a half than in my whole life - I've been in the United Kingdom for 10 years but I've learned more since coming here than I did before. I've been given the opportunities to do things and become successful and improve my life. I tell the women: 'Don't just sit in your house. Do something for yourself!' In our culture, women only think about their families and not themselves. I want to set up a men's project too. Women can learn and understand but still might not be allowed to do anything so we need to work with the men too. We need to change their minds that women can go to work, learn English – so the limits for the women can go. It is better for all of us when women can do these things.

Ramineh – From Housewife to Entrepreneur

I started coming to the women's project a year ago. My friend was coming here and told me about it. I've been in the United Kingdom for seven years but since coming here I have learned more about the law and my rights than before because I was always at home. I have learned new things. I can book GP and hairdresser's appointments, I can talk on the phone, fill in forms and write messages. I can read letters from my children's school. In the past, I didn't know about services available, how to go to the doctor. I didn't have the confidence to travel alone. I couldn't read the signs. Now I have travelled to visit my mother in Pakistan. It affects my children. I can help my children with their homework. We had a workshop on the school system. Now, I can understand what they need and how to support them. I have confidence. I can advise them and make sure I am involved in their lives. Before, my daughter would say 'Why can't you help?' Now, I can. I have shown my children you can change and learn. We had a workshop on volunteering and I learned that I could become a volunteer and gain work experience. With the help of the staff here, I learned how to volunteer. I cook here when they have groups in. I make food that people can afford and it makes a bit of money for the project and now they pay me a bit too. I'm doing a cooking qualification. I came here to learn and then I could begin to help and now I'm cooking and getting paid and fundraising. It's a small enterprise! I am very happy in my life. It's the first year since I've been in this country that I feel happy in myself. I know the law, my rights and how to get help. I see people from my country and other countries eating my food and complimenting me. I want to continue down this path of development and learning to assist my children and I want to start my own business. All the experience here is a step for me towards starting my own business.

Ramineh's story also featured heavily in staff and volunteer interviews:

> She is a young lady, in her twenties, with four children and a passion for cooking. She started by making baked Afghan goods and selling them to volunteers in the office. Then she started an initiative where she cooks lunch every day that people are here and we sell it to staff, volunteers, the local community and local businesses. I've seen her confidence grow so much. She used to be

so shy and now she will answer questions about how to make the
food and will ask people how it is. She has a source of income and a
sense of agency.

(Sarah, project worker)

She's doing something with her skills. She thought she would always
be at home. She's had driving lessons and learned how to drive too.
Seeing women become staff and volunteers is the most memorable
impact for me.

(Nahar, volunteer)

It's been a big change in her life - both in terms of financial
independence and speaking up. She says her husband now
questions her less and gives her more freedom.

(Aminah, project worker)

JOURNEYS OF CHANGE

The women's project supported many of the women who engaged with it over
the three years to become more empowered and make changes to their lives. In
years one and two, the changes to their lives were manifested in the women
feeling safe, being less isolated, building positive relationships with each other
and with staff and volunteers, implementing healthy changes to their lifestyles,
making progress in learning English, accessing services independently and
engaging with their children's education. In year three, more substantial
and sustainable changes have included taking on volunteering roles, paid
employment and further study.

In years two and three of the project, some women presented workshops to
their peers. This not only empowered the women presenting but also those
who observed them. Other women attending the project have taken on other
volunteering and paid roles for the charity. This development into role models
sustains the model of engagement where women are supported by other
women they can relate to. Examples of this are seen in the case studies presented above including the project coordinator, Mojdeh, who was a refugee
herself as well as Fatima, Firouzeh and Ramineh who became volunteers and

staff in year three of the project. The 'journey of change' many of the women moved through is represented by Fig. 2.

The women's engagement and participation developed over time. Initially, many attended the project to learn English or found the charity while looking

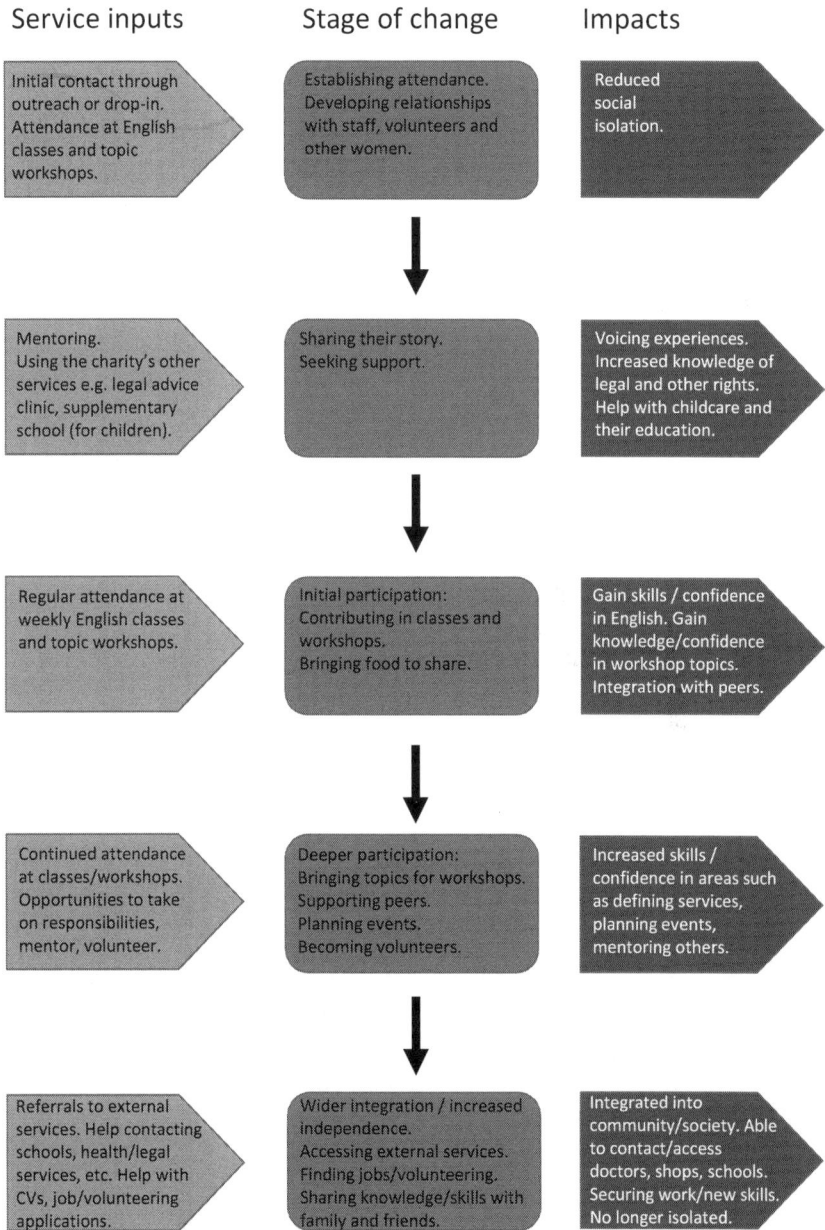

Service inputs	Stage of change	Impacts
Initial contact through outreach or drop-in. Attendance at English classes and topic workshops.	Establishing attendance. Developing relationships with staff, volunteers and other women.	Reduced social isolation.
Mentoring. Using the charity's other services e.g. legal advice clinic, supplementary school (for children).	Sharing their story. Seeking support.	Voicing experiences. Increased knowledge of legal and other rights. Help with childcare and their education.
Regular attendance at weekly English classes and topic workshops.	Initial participation: Contributing in classes and workshops. Bringing food to share.	Gain skills / confidence in English. Gain knowledge/confidence in workshop topics. Integration with peers.
Continued attendance at classes/workshops. Opportunities to take on responsibilities, mentor, volunteer.	Deeper participation: Bringing topics for workshops. Supporting peers. Planning events. Becoming volunteers.	Increased skills / confidence in areas such as defining services, planning events, mentoring others.
Referrals to external services. Help contacting schools, health/legal services, etc. Help with CVs, job/volunteering applications.	Wider integration / increased independence. Accessing external services. Finding jobs/volunteering. Sharing knowledge/skills with family and friends.	Integrated into community/society. Able to contact/access doctors, shops, schools. Securing work/new skills. No longer isolated.

Fig. 2. The Women's Project 'Journey of Change'.

for support with a specific issue related to their status as migrants or refugees. Ongoing support enabled them to share their broader stories and get support with a more holistic range of needs. Over time, as women got to know each other, they began to participate by bringing food to share, supporting each other with English and interpretation. Some of the women who engaged long-term were able to build the knowledge and confidence to deliver workshops and become role models to their peers.

The third year of the women's project saw more women implementing more substantial changes to their lives such as gaining volunteering experience and even paid work. This is in part due to having improved their English language skills over time as well as some having accessed the project with higher levels of English than in previous years. Learning English remained a fundamental catalyst for integration for the women. In year three, women accessed the project at different levels in the diagram in Fig. 2, with many of them having felt the benefit of continued attendance at English classes and workshops over time. Several of the core group of women attending in year three engaged in volunteering, further study, or even secured paid work, as in the case of Ramineh outlined earlier. This demonstrates them becoming more integrated into society, and in some cases moving beyond the women's project.

Staff and volunteers also recognised there were challenges to integration faced by some women. One of the project workers reflected that becoming integrated is a slow and limited process for the most isolated women:

> *You could say that integration is less successful if we're talking about the women whose starting point is lowest, they are not really engaging with those from other cultures.*
>
> *(Sarah, project worker)*

However, as in previous years, this was couched in the recognition that even small steps towards being more socially integrated were significant for the most isolated women and that the cultural relatability of the project was also a strength. These women often faced multiple barriers to integration including lack of English, cultural restrictions and mental health problems.

> *There are examples of women who don't go to anything else but come to the women's project. They've made friends and it can be the only time they leave the house to do something for themselves rather than their husbands or children. Even if they are not yet registered to vote or achieving English qualifications, the soft outcomes are massive outcomes for them. The higher-level ability women have the*

confidence that leads to integration outcomes like university study. For those with little English, their starting point is very low.

(Sarah, project worker)

Across the interviews, the volunteers and participants identified that for some women, they had been extremely isolated before coming to the women's project. One of the former participants who had recently become a volunteer stated:

We need to give them hope and inspiration. They are only at home with their kids. They forget themselves. They need to know that there are opportunities for them. There is a lot of depression. We need to help them open up and ask for help.

(Samaneh, volunteer)

For the women with the lowest starting points, their progress through the journey of change was necessarily slow and not yet complete, and relied on holistic and consistent support.

The project workers and volunteers recognised the importance of long-term support and relationships in supporting the women's engagement.

Whenever there has been a leader leaving or a birthday, the women are brilliant and turn up with cakes and presents. They get real pleasure from celebrating each other and their achievements. On International Women's Day, we all wrote cards to each other and read them out. It shows the strength of the bond between volunteers and participants.

(Sarah, project worker)

They also recognised the disruptions to this when staff or volunteers changed or provision was moved or paused.

The women continued to be aspirational and spoke of their long-term hopes and ambitions for the future in their interviews and were confident they were on the way to achieving these. For example, Taara stated:

Coming here has helped me, it's given me experience. I'm now studying Health and Social Care level three. I'm going to be a social worker, midwife or nurse. I know I want to work with people. I have so many options.

(Taara, volunteer)

The staff and volunteers also recognised that the women's aspirations had grown and felt achievable in the third year of the project. For example, one of the project workers stated:

> *They aspire higher – they are more ambitious. They want to enter further education or employment where it wasn't in their plans before. They are inspired by others.*
>
> *(Aminah, project worker)*

This demonstrates that in year three, there were still examples of women whose empowerment was still aspirational or only just becoming tangible. Some of the women, however, who had been engaged with the project long-term, such as those in the case studies above, had moved through and reached the later stages of the journey of change and achieved significant change in their lives.

CONCLUSIONS

The women's project aimed to engage marginalised migrant and refugee women, to support them to make changes in their lives, and become more empowered and integrated. This was supported through the provision of workshops, English classes, as well as individual support and social solidarity. The workshops were the central feature of the women's project (and, indeed, what its funding was focused on) but they cannot be separated from the range of holistic provision that formed the overall experience for the women who took part.

Across the three years of the women's project, 97% of the women attending stated that the workshops were relevant to their lives, 92% reported increased knowledge through the workshops, and 93% said they would do something differently in their lives as a result of the workshops. This was manifested in the women's empowerment across the three years which developed and became more significant over time. In the first year of the project, the women's empowerment was largely aspirational with them stating a desire for increased confidence, skills, knowledge, wellbeing and freedom – and starting to take steps towards these such as taking English classes and attending informational workshops on topics such as driving, CV-writing, the UK education system and parenting skills. In year two, more tangible change was becoming manifested with the women feeling safer and less isolated, becoming more engaged in their children's education, and making strides in learning English. In year three of the project, the women made the most significant and long-term changes to their lives including engaging in further study at college and university, learning to drive, taking on volunteering roles and, for some, securing paid employment. These significant changes tended to be made by the women who had been engaged with the project for at least a year, many for much longer. The case studies in this chapter illustrate some of these stories of empowerment.

In year three, as in previous years, some limits to integration emerged, as seen in the quotations from project workers above where they reflect on the small steps made and varied starting points for many of the women. Not all the women taking part in year three were engaged since the beginning of the project or even for more than a few months. As with all community work based on voluntary participation, attendance and engagement was fluctuating for many women with different core groups forming at different times. Disruptions to staffing, location, and frequency of provision affected engagement and highlighted again the precarity of support for migrant and refugee women being under-funded, provided 'in kind' and on a voluntary basis. However, formalising such work would present its own challenges and the women's project being grassroots and bottom-up, rather than top-down and policy-defined, was also a strength.

The women's project deepened its women-led peer support in year three through several women taking on substantial volunteering and staff roles for the charity. Through these volunteering opportunities, the women made significant steps towards their own integration goals as well as being role models that other women could relate to. Staff and volunteers also identified benefits to themselves of being involved with the women's project. Aminah explained in interview 'I'm much more confident in professional and social contexts' and others had similar comments. This is significant given so many of them were former participants in the project and the opportunities to volunteer with the charity supported them to gain skills and experience towards their own integration goals.

As in years one and two, the success of the project rested on the provision of an accessible and safe, culturally-sensitive, women-only space in which to access a range of support relevant to the women's lives. The opportunities for women to take on volunteering and staff roles sustained this model of grassroots provision. These staff and volunteers were not only relatable role models but also understood the needs of their peers. This led, for example, to a focus on mental health rather than just practical workshops in year three of the project, an often hidden and neglected issue among refugee women that impacts on their ability to be fully integrated and empowered.

The focus on mental health across several workshops in year three enabled the women to begin to recognise trauma in their lives, and its impact. The next chapter explores in more detail the importance of trauma-informed practice with migrant and refugee women. It looks back at the experiences of trauma that emerged in the qualitative data across the three years, and reflects on the 'body and mind' workshops delivered in year three of the project.

8

TRAUMA-INFORMED PRACTICE WITH MIGRANT AND REFUGEE WOMEN

This chapter explores the need for a trauma-informed approach in work with women from refugee and migrant backgrounds, who may have experienced multiple traumas including displacement, isolation, violence and abuse, and health trauma, among others. The women's project largely focused on workshops to provide practical information and skills in years one and two but this fell short of providing a way to recognise and address the trauma of their experiences. In year three, more emphasis was placed on mental health and well-being. In this context, we were able to pilot two 'body and mind' workshops that used art and movement therapeutic methods. The chapter outlines the experiences of trauma that emerged in the narratives of the women over the three-year project. We argue that mental health and trauma are neglected in policy and practice with migrant and refugee groups and that trauma-informed practice needs to be more embedded in such work. Holistic and intersectional research and practice cannot ignore trauma and its impact, if it is to engage with the whole experience of migrant and refugee women and understand how their different experiences intersect.

We recognise the limitations of talking approaches in research and practice for exploring traumatic trajectories with groups who have limited English. Additionally, for women who have had complex experiences and experienced abuse and displacement, talking and asking questions is a limited method to take this further. The chapter considers the potential of creative therapeutic methods, with refugee and migrant women and draws on observational reflections from the 'body and mind' workshops. These workshops were facilitated by a dance movement psychotherapist (Rova) and observed by the academic researcher (Thompson) and also attended by some of the practitioner-researchers at the women's project.

Trauma-informed practice has gained traction in social and community services in recent years and there has been a greater recognition of the impact of trauma in the lives of service-users across a range of sectors, but particularly in work with children and young people. Trauma-informed practice is defined by SAMHSA (2014) as services that are able to, firstly, work with their user groups in ways that 'realise' the impact of trauma. Secondly, staff in such services should be able to 'recognise' and 'respond' to generalised and individual presentations of trauma. Thirdly, they must 'resist' re-traumatisation or inflicting further trauma. Finally, they play a part in supporting their clients towards 'recovery' from trauma and its effects on their lives.

As demonstrated in the preceding chapters, the women's project appeared to have begun to recognise and respond to such trauma, particularly by year three (see Chapter 7). Certain key principles underpin the trauma-informed approach, these being: safety; trustworthiness and transparency; peer support opportunities; collaboration and mutuality; empowerment, voice and choice; recognition of cultural, historical and gender issues (SAMHSA, 2014). These principles reflect those that appear to have been embedded in the practice of the women's project, particularly supporting women's empowerment through providing a safe space, peer support, and recognising the impact of cultural and gender issues. This suggests the trauma-informed approach would fit well with their ways of working. These principles also intersect with the values of community development more broadly (CLD Standards Council, 2021; ESB, 2015).

Whilst a trauma-informed approach has become more formally embedded in some areas of UK policy and practice, for example in youth justice, it has been largely neglected in integration policy and practice. The lack of policy direction and funding for embedding a trauma-informed approach in work with migrant and refugee communities is problematic, given the vast and varied experiences of trauma faced by displaced groups. A lack of funding for community mental health services more broadly, and barriers faced by migrant and refugee women in accessing mainstream services, compound a lack of attention to the mental health of these women.

While a focus on overcoming trauma could be criticised for reflecting a neoliberal focus on people's deficits and individual problems, there is arguably a need to recognise the impacts of the traumas experienced by refugee and migrant groups in community development interventions. Umer and Elliott (2021) in their study of refugees' post-traumatic growth, suggest fostering hope is crucial to promote refugee integration into society. This supports our argument that both strengths and challenges should be recognised and addressed as part of a balanced model of practice that incorporates both the needs and assets of marginalised groups (see Chapter 4). Additionally, it has been argued that a holistic trauma-informed approach recognises structural and institutional trauma alongside individual trauma (Brennan, Bush, Trickey, Levene, & Watson, 2019; Spacey & Thompson, 2021). The impact of institutional and structural trauma is highly relevant for refugee and migrant women, who often experience intersectional oppressions and violence before, during and beyond their displacement.

TRAUMA-INFORMED PRACTICE WITH REFUGEE AND MIGRANT COMMUNITIES

According to research published in the Journal of Affective Disorders 'migration is considered a depression risk factor when associated with psychosocial adversity' (Saraga, Gholam-Rezaee, & Preisig, 2013, p. 795). Furthermore, '[i]n patients meeting (diagnostic) criteria for major depressive disorder, clinical presentation in migrants was characterized by a high number of comorbid diagnoses, especially anxiety disorders, somatoform disorders and post-traumatic stress disorders, and a chronic, severe, unremitting course' (Saraga et al., 2013, p. 795). While diagnostic specification of trauma is defined by actual or threatened death, serious injury, or sexual violence (American Psychiatric Association, DSM V, 2013), there are additional events and experiences in the journey of a migrant that arguably cause serious psychological harm or indeed trauma, including separation from family and children, social isolation, unemployment and homelessness to name a few. In his seminal book *The Body Keeps the Score* van der Kolk (2014, p. 203) explains:

> *Nobody can 'treat' a war, or abuse, rape, molestation, or any other horrendous event, for that matter; what has happened cannot be undone. But what can be dealt with are the imprints of trauma on body, mind and soul: the crushing sensations in your chest that you may label as anxiety or depression; the fear of losing control; always being on alert for danger or rejection; the self-loathing; the nightmares and flashbacks; the fog that keeps you from staying on task and from engaging fully in what you are doing; being unable to fully open your heart to another human being.*

van der Kolk proposes that holistic recovery from trauma must be built on the following coping strategies (1) dealing with hyperarousal, (2) developing self-awareness, (3) building meaningful relationships, (4) being part of a community and (5) using touch for safe physical boundaries. Physical and psychological trauma is often incomprehensible and difficult to put into words. For the refugee and migrant population, language is thus doubly limiting as a medium of expressing and processing trauma.

Vromans et al. (2017) suggest that loss is often an invisible factor of trauma distress, but they distinguish traumatic loss from grief (the 'normal' experience of bereavement) and cultural bereavement (loss linked to displacement). Loss may be a universal experience. However, the multiplicity of how it is experienced, expressed and processed individually and culturally is socio-politically complex. Therefore, the meaning attributed to experiences of loss by women themselves must be taken into consideration in the context of trauma recovery and mental health.

Meaning-making seems to play an integral part not only in the articulation of trauma but also in reconstructing one's identity after the trauma experience. Recovery from trauma thus is also contextualised as post-traumatic growth, 'a process of transformation, in which survivors develop beyond their pre-crisis level of adaptation and psychological functioning' (Uy & Okubo, 2018, p. 220) through a process of restructuring their trauma narrative. Similarly, in considering involuntary migration, Papadopoulos (2021) develops five key narrative themes: home, identity, nostalgic disorientation, victimisation and trauma. He explores these narratives as central to the lived experience of migration and calls for synergic therapeutic approaches that take into account a person's capacity for adversity-activated development.

Unlike trauma sufferers whose trauma may have occurred in the past (see war veterans) for some refugees and migrants, trauma is an enduring experience influenced by structural and situated factors including employment, economic and socio-political stressors (Goodman, Vesely, Letiecq, & Cleavelant, 2017). In this sense, both internal (individual resources) and external processes (governmental and systemic structures) are essential towards fostering recovery from trauma and resilience. Access to resources, such as healthcare, education and employment must be considered alongside individual cultural needs including faith and religious practices. Outreach work, partnership networks among service providers, and community research are thought to be effective ways towards bridging gaps in resources (Goodman et al., 2017). However, trauma-informed work alone is insufficient in addressing migrant women's long-term distress induced by post-settlement financial difficulties (O'Donnell, Stuart, & O'Donnell, 2020). Not only must these stressors be identified by care or community engagement providers but interventions must be centred on them.

MOVEMENT AND ART THERAPY METHODS WITH REFUGEE AND MIGRANT COMMUNITIES

The arts therapies are psychotherapeutic approaches that utilise creative artistic processes to support individuals or groups to work through relational psychological material. In the UK there are four distinct disciplines; dance movement psychotherapy, art psychotherapy, drama therapy and music therapy, with their own professional bodies, accreditation and postgraduate training routes. Arts therapists may also work cross-modally, for example combining two or more approaches to facilitate the therapeutic process. Therapeutic treatment provision is usually part of a multi-disciplinary service pathway delivered through primary (physical health), secondary (mental health) or voluntary sector (charity) organisations. However, for the migrant population, access to therapy is not a straightforward process as many find themselves in limbo due to their status and limited legal rights as asylum seekers or refugees. In the absence of therapy provision, engagement with artistic practice may also include non-clinical interventions such as community arts projects. As outlined by the UK Government's review of the evidence for arts-based social prescribing (Fancourt, Warran, & Aughterson, 2020), it is thought that engagement with the arts may contribute to aspects of social cohesion, improve well-being in adults, reduce social inequalities, improve educational attainment and help manage, treat and prevent mental illness, among other benefits.

Arts therapy practitioners have been supporting refugee and migrant populations across the different stages of their migration journey since the beginning of the century. The immediacy and accessibility of arts therapies are acknowledged as effective therapeutic approaches for the therapeutic needs of migrant and refugee communities (Dokter, 1998). Artistic practice is able to traverse language barriers, given engagement with the creative process is not reliant on verbal communication. Importantly, creative therapeutic processes enable participants to connect with current lived experience, past trauma, thoughts and feelings at a felt (or else experiential) level. Working through distressing material creatively helps participants to integrate previously marginalised or fragmented parts of themselves, offering possibilities for psychological growth and repair. The transformative experience of creative process then acts as a metaphor for participants' internal and external transformative restoration.

In her book chapter 'In Limbo', Callaghan (1998) explored the re-enactment of traumatic lived experience within a movement psychotherapy group with adult male refugees and asylum seekers: 'The effect of being suspended in limbo and the realities of refugee life are replayed in the therapy through absences, disappearances and unresolved endings... Feelings of persecution and hostility, loss and isolation permeate the process' (p. 39). The group participants were thus able to articulate traumatic experiences in practice and work on repairing fragmented parts of themselves through the relational creative process: 'The all-pervasive sense of limbo that refugees experience is reflected in and can be transformed through the dual nature of movement, not only as a continuous process of becoming but also as a position reached' (p. 39).

The importance of re-building a sense of personhood is also articulated in Jimerson's (2017) 're-painting self' project, an art therapy provision exploring ontological security with traumatised refugee children. Here, art-making supported not only the meaning-making (making sense) of lived experience but contributed to its reconstitution (potential for transformation). Further evidence on the efficacy of creative arts therapy in improving migrant well-being is provided by García-Medrano and Panhofer (2020) through their two-year study with 51 migrants and asylum seekers living in Glasgow. The researchers reported that the use of spontaneous movement as part of a dance movement psychotherapy intervention increased participants' well-being, sense of confidence and social integration.

Creative movement and art have also been combined as part of an open therapeutic space service for refugee and asylum-seeking women living in temporary accommodation (Rova, Burrell, & Cohen, 2020). The Moving Space therapists described how working alongside the women, allowed them to come closer to the shared journeys in a non-intrusive manner:

> *Journeying through the transient space of the group, the women's explorations evoke both a realisation of loss (of who and what they have left behind) and a hope for the future (having survived the journey so far). The creative process thus, becomes a steppingstone towards the women's articulation of both these experiences. The cross-modality approach offers an opportunity for participants to tap into vulnerable feelings and reconnect with the ground (through the embodied explorations) and to visualise coherent and incoherent aspects of their story (through the art making). The group offers a vehicle to visit past and future journeys, a forum to discover new languages and to experience one's self differently in the exploration of unfolding identity, cultural interplay and the co-creation of meaning.*
>
> *(Rova et al., 2020, p. 211)*

Hanania (2018) wrote about the importance of a creative and culturally informed treatment of trauma for Syrian refugee women. The author identified a gap in culturally appropriate therapeutic provision and, in response, adapted art therapy through expressive embroidery work to support the needs of this group of refugee women. Here, embroidery, a culturally acceptable practice, was utilised therapeutically allowing women to weave their stories safely and discreetly.

The importance of culturally informed therapy interventions is echoed in Conner's (2020) music therapy research which focused on refugees in the Mexican-US border. The author suggested that there is an overemphasis on the trauma experience of refugees, which can be a disempowering label as it takes away the individual's unique resources and identity. Conner (2020) calls for the development of culturally 'humble music therapy practices' that go beyond the expression of trauma in Western terms:

> *Music, if allowed, can provide a space for people to make bold claims about their sense of belonging and experienced racially inflected nationalism. This space becomes even more salient and effective when the music holding these claims is of the culture being represented.*
>
> *(p. 13)*

Therefore, in working with refugee and asylum-seeking women, we must continue to stay alert to potential cultural, socio-political and relational power dynamics enacted within the creative, therapeutic and community spaces that we invite them into, lest we contribute to their ongoing traumatisation.

REFUGEE AND MIGRANT WOMEN'S EXPERIENCE OF TRAUMA

As we highlighted in Chapter 3, refugee and migrant women have often experienced traumatic trajectories, in life in their home countries, their displacement and migration journeys, as well as after 'settling' in a new country. At times throughout the three years of the women's project, the women's experiences of trauma, past and present, emerged in their interview narratives. This trauma was related to a range of experiences including their displacement as well as in experiences of prejudice and discrimination, domestic violence, isolation and health problems.

While the interviews focused on the women's life in the UK, they often drew on their experiences of and reasons for migration as part of this context. From this, some indication of the trauma of displacement emerged such as separation from family and arriving in the UK alone, as in the two examples below from the case studies in Chapter 7.

> *Because of my work supporting women's rights I had to flee the Taliban. I fled to India in 2012 and came to the UK in 2015, with no English language and without my husband and children – they arrived later.*
>
> (Mojdeh, project coordinator, year three)

> *I am from Syria and was a refugee in Lebanon before coming to the UK through the UN resettlement scheme two years ago... I used to be scared... When I moved to London, I felt scared and alone.*
>
> (Habiba, year three participant)

One of the main forms of trauma experienced by the women once they arrived in the UK was the trauma of isolation. In interviews, this was a prevalent theme that emerged particularly in years one and two of the project (see Chapters 5 and 6).

> *I started from zero. I felt blind and dumb, not able to speak. I felt so depressed because I was feeling if I see someone in the street, what will I say? I was scared of communication.*
>
> (Razia, year one participant)

> *If I go shopping, everywhere, if I can't speak with people, you feel indifferent, no one talks to you, you don't have friends because you don't speak the same language.*
>
> (Fariba, year one participant)

> *I only stayed at home and took my children to school. I felt isolated, on my own.*
>
> (Gulzar, year two participant)

These examples show how the trauma of isolation compounded the fear and lack of confidence that would have enabled the women to make steps to overcome it. These experiences likely produced typical trauma responses such as 'freezing', 'flopping' or 'fleeing' (Lodrick, 2007). Such responses may have led to the women both avoiding situations that would have made them less isolated (the fleeing response), and feeling unable to take positive action towards changing their circumstances (freezing and flopping). A fear of their new context, a lack of knowledge of UK systems and services, and a lack of English language in particular compounded this isolation for many of the women.

> I want to go shopping without being scared. I want to go to the doctor without someone else there. I have the coil – I couldn't tell my daughter because I'm embarrassed. I had an interpreter. I dream of the day I can talk to the doctor without telling someone else. I wasn't sure the interpreter got it right... Once I wanted to buy spinach. I went into the shop three times, I had to go home and get the empty bag.
>
> (Nargis, year one participant)

This isolation and the impact on the women's mental health was also recognised by project staff and volunteers in interviews, as well as them identifying how the women rarely had space to focus on their own needs. They saw a key part of their role, as an organisation working towards women's integration, as providing a space for women to both be with each other and to focus on themselves.

> We need to give them hope and inspiration. They are only at home with their kids. They forget themselves. They need to know that there are opportunities for them. There is a lot of depression. We need to help them open up and ask for help.
>
> (Samaneh, volunteer, year three)

The women's project participants and staff also reflected on how prejudice and harassment experienced by the women in public impacted on their lives. The trauma of such experiences of hate and discrimination emerged in interviews and reflections.

> The women have told us how they have been targets of bullying and harassment and how wearing a headscarf makes them a particular target for discrimination in public or when trying to access services or work... They face unique challenges to maintain their identity while seeking to succeed in a new society.
>
> (Charity director, year two)

> One day I was walking with three friends and a man spat on us and told us to go home and that we were all immigrants. I didn't do anything because I thought the police would want evidence... I didn't

go out for a long time after it happened and I didn't want my
daughter to see it but she was there.

(Soraya, year two participant)

Some women also recounted experiences of abuse at home and escaping violent relationships. The trauma of abuse emerged in Gulzar's (Chapter 6) and Fatima's (Chapter 7) narratives and compounded other traumas such as isolation and fear of life in the UK.

There is a restrictive order placed on my husband... He didn't let me
take part in activities and being outside the home. He stopped me
having money and told me who I could talk to.

(Gulzar, year two participant)

I suffered from domestic violence. My husband totally broke my
confidence... I'm a single mum with no help.

(Fatima, year three participant)

Other traumas also emerged in interviews that impacted on overall experiences of trauma. For example, trauma of illness compounded negative feelings and contributed to experiences of depression and mental ill health.

I had heart surgery last year... I'm thirty and I've been ill for five
years. I've sometimes felt depressed because of my illness... All I've
done for six years is walk to the nursery and school and back.

(Mariam, year one participant)

Such experiences demonstrate how such issues are interconnected, creating overlapping and intersectional traumas; for example, in Mariam's case, her physical illness impacted on her mental health and level of isolation.

Whilst the women in our research have shown great resilience, they also experienced many traumas, and these require a trauma-informed approach. This needs to be couched in the recognition that many of their traumas were institutional and structural and will have impacted on their ability to access services, particularly those that reflect the institutions that abused them. The charity director's and Soraya's comments above suggest that institutional traumas are being recognised in the women's project. The need for a trauma-informed approach supports our argument that a focus on recognising needs and on overcoming challenges is required for the most marginalised (and, indeed, traumatised) groups, as well as fostering a hopeful practice that builds on their assets and potential.

The women recognised the need to focus more on their mental health and experiences of trauma after the 'body and mind' workshops as well as after workshops on stress and mental health, as shown in the workshop evaluations in the third year of the project (see Chapter 7).

> *I didn't think about myself and my mind before.*

> *As a woman I need to think about myself as well as my family.*

> *A really good workshop for refugee women and those of us who have travelled to the UK. It really helped with mental health and knowing how to get support.*

> *We learned about the small steps we can take to feel better. I liked learning about 'grounding'. I will try this at home when I am feeling worried.*

These comments reflect the importance of developing trauma-informed interventions with migrant and refugee women.

Trauma-informed community work requires long-term support, rather than short-term or ad hoc interventions. Aminah, one of the project workers interviewed in year three recognised that over time 'the women have become more open to talking about personal and sensitive issues and trauma'. This needs to be built on with further work to explore and address the impact of these traumas.

Whilst the research interviews quoted in this section focused primarily on the women's experiences in the UK since displacement from their home country, the pilot 'body and mind' workshops in year three allowed the women to express experiences from both before, during and after their migration journeys in a more holistic and creative process than the interviews allowed for. These workshops and their impact are explored below.

THE 'BODY AND MIND' WORKSHOPS

The 'body and mind' creative workshops in year three of the women's project were designed for women to explore and share their stories of forced migration with an emphasis on the impact of displacement on their mental health and well-being. The connection between embodied relational experience and mental processing ran through the creative workshops; thus 'body and mind' was selected as the working title for the pilot. Given the short-term nature of the provision (two sessions), we were mindful of the ethical considerations arising when structuring the creative workshops for this group of refugee women.

Even though the creative workshops held space for women to share their stories of migration, the work was not therapy as such in that it did not focus on unpacking individual and group process material. Rather, the focus of the sessions was on acknowledging the psychological impact of the experience of migration on the individual and the community more broadly. Through the sharing and witnessing of each other's stories creatively, the sessions allowed the women to normalise and de-stigmatise their experiences of trauma, mental distress and displacement via a process of mutual recognition and validation of their lived experiences.

Another ethical consideration involved the issue of consent for their participation due to the language barrier. In addition, the importance of developing a culturally appropriate creative process was considered. We may refer to these women as a group of refugee women, but of course their cultural, religious and socio-political diversity highlights that they are not one homogenous group and what might be culturally appropriate for one participant might not be so for another. The way we navigated these tensions was by combining structure with free association as part of the creative explorations. The women were invited to participate in creative tasks clearly outlined and demonstrated by the facilitator through verbal (speaking) and non-verbal (moving) explanations. The facilitator held the overall group process and time boundary and guided the exploration. Each participant then had the choice of bringing as much or as little of their story into the process as they felt able and safe to do so. The role of the facilitator here was key in calibrating the intensity of the work. Some women took their time to find their way into the group space, tentatively making a contribution and sharing their creative work. Other women readily offloaded their story with an urgency and emotional resonance that, if not sensitively contained, risked overwhelming the individual and the group.

To further anchor and contain the unfolding creative process, grounding techniques were introduced at the beginning and end of each workshop allowing participants to ease themselves into the creative work and complete their process respectively. These grounding exercises, which included guided breathing and body scans whilst attending to felt sensations, also served as self-regulation tools for participants to take forward into their everyday life as a way of managing stress and anxiety.

A final layer of safe practice embedded in this context involved the artwork created during the workshops. As the authors and narrators of their stories, women were empowered to decide what they wanted to do with the work created during the workshops. Some women perceived the work as a task completed within the boundaries of the workshop and thus were happy to leave it behind for the facilitator to dispose of. Other women resonated with their art object at a symbolic level and thus chose to take it with them to either display at home or continue working on in their own time. The symbolic significance of what women chose to take with them or leave behind resonated with their individual migrant story and this was acknowledged as a shared narrative in the sessions.

The First Workshop

In the first workshop, the focus was on connecting to personal narrative through felt sense exploration and visual storytelling. The group was set up around a large table in the activity room with women sitting in a circle. This group formation supported working alongside each other whilst keeping to our own space boundary. The structure of the table was an important feature for the introduction of the creative work. A parallel with gathering around the table for a feast may be drawn here. Interestingly, while the workshop was taking place a community lunch was being cooked (by Ramineh, see Chapter 7) on the floor below us, which women and their families were invited to after the session. The structure of the table and chairs provided not only scaffolding and support for the women's bodies but also a symbolic container for their emerging stories which were literally and metaphorically laid on the table.

After an initial round of introductions, greeting each other with different hand gestures and in different languages, the facilitator displayed a collection of postcards and photographs on the table with images of landscapes, portraits or abstract artwork. The women were invited to take some time to explore the images and then select a few that resonated with them. In their own work-space, women then constructed a visual narrative of their story and took turns to share in the group. Though the women were seemingly engaged in the same activity, the multiplicity by which they chose to symbolically articulate their story was striking. One member chose a single image of the portrait of a woman. Another participant was drawn to images of bridges recalling the many crossings she had had to make. Some connected to images of buildings or neighbourhoods, of what once they called home. Others chose a range of images to depict the different stages of their migration journey: life before fleeing the homeland, the treacherous journey to the foreign land and their experiences of resettlement.

One by one the women shared their story through their selected images, while the rest of the group watched and listened. Women held up their images, sometimes using words to explain why they had chosen them, sometimes gesturing to clarify important details such as specific colours or shapes. Women were also encouraged to sit with their story, simply looking at the images whilst noticing their affective responses at a somatic level. During the individual storytelling, the facilitator paid attention to participants' non-verbal expression of their narrative. The way women moved (held their posture, breathed, used their personal kinesphere) whilst telling their story revealed the impact the events they spoke of have had at a physical and mental level. Very soon, the group discussion moved to the somatisation (physical manifestations) of trauma. The women spoke about their experiences of chronic pain, migraines, sleep difficulties, anxiety and depression.

For the next part of the workshop, the women were supported to pay attention to their bodily sensations during a guided body scan exercise. Using small massage balls and the use of self-touch, women traced their body boundary, attending to areas of tension or stiffness. As we worked our way through the different parts, joints and muscles of the body, women spoke about their experiences of trauma this time through their moving body. The facilitator tracked the shared process by reflecting back to the group the verbal and non-verbal narratives emerging. The shared narratives of body memory, personhood and identity, femininity and loss echoed around the group.

The workshop closed with a grounding breathing exercise, and a group reflection on the link between thinking and feeling and the importance of considering our experiences holistically. The women commented on the sense of belonging they had experienced in the group and spoke about an inner calmness as the session ended.

The Second Workshop

The second workshop allowed for a more in-depth exploration of movement improvisation as an expressive tool. In addition, building from the visual storytelling from the first workshop, the women developed individual storyboards using collage work. Two work spaces were created in the activity room. The large table and chairs remained, with the inclusion of an open movement space which allowed for whole-body movement exploration. After the initial check-in around the table, the women were invited into the open space forming a circle in order to move together. Even this seemingly simple transition from the table to the open space evoked strong reactions in some participants. The metaphor of the sea (swimming in the deep) and a fear of the unknown emerged as the starting points of the shared exploration.

The group then negotiated a difference in preference regarding the use of music during the movement improvisation as some participants wanted to have music and others did not. This dilemma instigated a discussion around cultural norms and codes specifically in relation to women's position in different societies. Some participants explained that music and dancing were not socially acceptable activities for women in their culture. Others felt empowered to express themselves through singing and dancing in the privacy of the group. The group decided to explore movement without music initially. Participants were invited to contribute a movement (gesture, action or shape) as part of a co-created group dance. Each time, participants were asked to say a few words about their chosen movement, describing the action or incorporating sound or sharing what it reminded them of.

Movements from folk dances, recalled from childhood, or relating to womanhood and femininity were evoked during this part of the session. A strong sense of 'sisterhood' was expressed in the group as women shared birth stories, spoke about ageing bodies or lactating breasts and found release through laughing together. Eventually, the individual movements participants brought were linked together to form a dance which the group performed to an instrumental piece of music, with the agreement of the group. What was particularly noticeable during this second workshop, was that the full-body movement exploration enabled women to bring more of their personal material into the group, their voice and personality more confidently present in the space.

After the movement exploration, the group returned to the table and used collage materials to create individual storyboards. Women used diverse techniques to create their elaborate storyboards using magazine cut-outs, glitter, oil pastels, tracing techniques, charcoal, glue, wool and other craft materials. After completing their collage, the group walked around the table witnessing each other's work. The session ended with a group reflection on the session and women shared what they were taking from the 'body and mind' workshops overall.

Themes Emerging from the Creative Workshops

Considering the two workshops as a whole, three broad themes may be distinguished as overlapping narratives in the group process: (1) the somatisation of loss, (2) reconstructing identity and (3) the transformative potential of creativity.

Not only was loss a central theme in the women's stories, it was also located bodily as women held their stomach or thoracic area, as they recounted traumatic events, which they then linked to their current experiences of anxiety, stress or depression. Women spoke about losing their home, their loved ones, but also their status as professional women in some cases. We may therefore consider these losses in the context of ontological insecurity. To lose everything that one knows, that one relies upon to build a future, is a serious existential threat. A woman trembled as she recounted her experience of sleeping rough in a country she did not know.

Women also gave great importance to their situated, contextual and gendered experiences of their displacement. Ascribed cultural rules followed their relocation. Arriving in a Western society, they also experienced a different kind of pressure: to integrate in their new community by standards that were often culturally discordant. Restructuring their identity and finding their own voice seemed an ongoing process for most women in the group. In the creative process, the theme of identity was particularly prominent during the collage work where women combined different layers of material, texture and media to compose their storyboards. In one example, the image of a temple was accompanied by images of nature, fashion and modern architecture, East and West co-existing in a unique and imaginative way. To be able to both reveal and integrate these different perspectives visually and creatively offers the possibility for such an integration to happen at a psychic level.

The transformative potential of creativity manifested in three particular ways during the creative workshops. Transcending the language barrier through non-verbal, interactive and artistic processes freed up the expression of thoughts and feelings and gave women permission to be playful and experimental. This, in turn, allowed participants to connect to what embodied practitioners may describe as (free) flow: a sense of kinetic continuity and release that moves beyond catharsis and which enables immersion in an uninterrupted creative process. Thus participants not only experienced themselves differently, but crucially, they imagined themselves differently. The shared experience fostered a sense of belonging and validation within the group.

'LOST IN TRANSLATION' CREATIVE METHODS IN RESEARCH WITH REFUGEE AND MIGRANT COMMUNITIES

Exploring and responding to trauma is as complex a process in research, if not more so, as it is in practice. Attention is needed to the ethics of informed consent and avoidance of harm. Talking-based research methods, as with talking therapies, have their limitations in research with migrant and refugee groups due to the complexities and sensitivities of discussing experiences of trauma, as well as the range of first languages among the sample group. The presence of interpreters as a middle-person in interviews, alongside the complexities of describing trauma, may have led to the women's experiences in our research being, at times, 'lost in translation' or unknowingly reinterpreted by the research team.

As such, creative and arts-based methods have potential for use in research with migrant and refugee groups, as well as in practice. Traditional research interviews have limitations in how far they enable holistic and creative expression, especially when working with trauma, and with communities for whom English language levels are low. Either the presence or the absence of an interpreter could inhibit the research, as the presence of an 'insider' can at times support or present a barrier to the interviewee being able to speak openly. As discussed in Chapter 2 in our consideration of researcher positionalities, levels of insider and outsider status are complex in themselves. Using creative research methods that offer more potential for research participants to own and shape the methods of communication, as well as allowing them more control over who is present and how far they rely on or choose to use them, is likely to only enhance such research. In exploring experiences of trauma, this is paramount as many of the participants' experiences will have involved a lack of control.

CONCLUSION

As explored earlier in this book, integration policy and practice tends towards short-term interventions focused on a narrow range of hard outcomes such as learning English and gaining employment. Such interventions, particularly by statutory services, have largely failed to take account of trauma and have not taken a trauma-informed approach in work with migrant and refugee groups. Similarly, where community projects focus only on practical information and skills, such as language learning and employability, they are not allowing migrant and refugee people to deal with the blocks and barriers to moving on with their lives that are products of their trauma.

The women's project recognised, over time, the need for mental health support for the refugee and migrant women it was engaging and was beginning to develop such work in year three. While it was still in the process of developing longer-term mental health support, it's broader work was clearly informed by the principles of trauma-informed practice highlighted in this chapter. Specifically, it was providing a place of safety, peer support, the opportunity to exercise choice and voice (often for the first time), leading to empowerment, all couched in the awareness of how intersectional cultural, gender and other issues impact on the women's lives (SAMHSA, 2014).

Statutory counselling and well-being services available to migrant and refugee women are underfunded. Where services are available, questions have been raised over their accessibility and cultural competence in engaging marginalised women who face intersectional oppressions, particularly around ethnicity, gender and religion (Nurein & Iqbal, 2021). A body of research and practice does exist that focuses on the potential for creative therapeutic methods in work with refugee women. This work has been shown to have clear efficacy, as demonstrated by the literature and practice explored in this chapter. Ensuring availability of such provision more consistently feels important in the context of this research with migrant and refugee women.

We argue for embedded and creative therapeutic approaches in broader community practices rather than disparate and disconnected services. There is a need for holistic and culturally sensitive services that take account of trauma in context. Marginalised refugee and migrant women who have experienced trauma need longer-term interventions with a consistent therapist rather than the more ad hoc workshops facilitated in year three of the women's project. These workshops scratched the surface of exploring the psychological impacts of their trajectories and were highly appreciated by the women in evaluations and interviews – but were too short-term to become therapeutic and to go beyond surfacing their trauma to begin to address its impacts. This, once again, reflects the precarity of funding for mental health community services and a reliance on an underfunded and patchy voluntary sector to bridge the gap.

The pilot 'body and mind' workshops, despite their limitations, were powerful and empowering – and some key themes emerged from the women's experiences through their creative process. These included: the manifestations of trauma in their current and physical experiences, impacting on their physical and mental health; the fracturing of their identities and the struggle to maintain them through their settlement (and the demands of a narrow integration agenda) in a Western country; and, finally, the transformative potential of longer-term creative methods of expression. These themes emphasise how the creative process has potential for both therapeutic practice with migrant and refugee women and also for research with them, enabling them to tell their stories in new and empowering ways, both collectively and individually.

Overall, the chapter demonstrates that holistic and intersectional research and practice with migrant and refugee women cannot ignore trauma and its impact. Within this, there is arguably a need to connect individual trauma with recognition of structural and institutional trauma (Brennan et al., 2019; Spacey & Thompson, 2021). The women's narratives, through the interviews and the creative 'body and mind' workshops, highlighted both their resilience and vulnerability, emphasising once again the need for a balanced model of practice that responds to both needs and assets. Within this, trauma-informed practice needs to encompass specific mental health interventions as well as being part of the overall approach to working with migrant and refugee women.

9

CONCLUSIONS AND IMPLICATIONS – DEVELOPING POLICY, PRACTICE AND RESEARCH WITH AND FOR MIGRANT AND REFUGEE WOMEN

In this final chapter, the key implications for policy, practice and research that have emerged from the preceding chapters are outlined. These implications emerge from the key arguments developed throughout the book from the research data. The chapter argues for an integrated model of practice for community work with refugee and migrant women that recognises their intersectional identities, experiences and oppressions. The research demonstrates that an integrated, bottom-up approach is successful in engaging isolated women and for facilitating their integration and empowerment. Within this, opportunities for English language learning and mental health support are key, alongside the development of knowledge capital and social solidarity. This is best supported by a balanced model of community development, that both responds to needs and recognises assets in its support of marginalised groups. Empowerment was found to be a long-term process with the qualitative data demonstrating that it first becomes manifested in aspirational goals before tangible and sustainable change are achieved over time.

Such forms of community development are precarious in that they are underfunded and not endorsed by policy-makers, who seek short-term solutions based on narrow understandings of integration. Tensions emerge where integration focuses on becoming 'more British' and migrant and refugee women are expected to meet hard outcomes such as paid employment while their unique lives, cultures and values are disregarded. Mental health issues within these communities are prevalent and it is crucial for practice to be trauma-informed and culturally sensitive, supporting our argument for a focus on needs as well as assets. Clear tensions emerge between a focus on women's empowerment and the barriers to this that are presented by structural factors, such as complex systems that exacerbate inequalities and marginalisation, as well as direct prejudice and discrimination in society.

The book has drawn out the implications and tensions that emerge from the research and these are summarised below. Overall, the case study of the women's project presents clear implications for both practice and research with migrant and refugee women, that emphasises the importance of centring their voices and involving them as insider-experts.

COMMUNITY DEVELOPMENT WITH MIGRANT AND REFUGEE WOMEN AS HOLISTIC AND INTERSECTIONAL

An intersectional perspective on refugee and migrant women's lives requires holistic provision – their lives, identities, challenges and assets cannot be broken down into separate issues for separate responses as they are fluid and overlapping, intertwined and complexly interrelated. The women's project case study demonstrates the importance of a holistic model of provision for migrant and refugee women, where they are able to access English language classes, practical workshops, mental health support, individual mentoring and social support. Together, these contribute to a holistic model of community development that recognises the importance of hard outcomes like learning English but equally, the importance of softer outcomes such as gaining knowledge, confidence and skills, setting goals and being supported to make broader changes in their lives.

While learning English remained a fundamental catalyst for empowerment and integration, the women's project recognised the limitations of focusing only on narrow indicators of the women becoming integrated, and its practice was centred on the delivery of practical workshops that developed broader knowledge and skills. English classes were often the initial draw for women's attendance and these were more informal, flexible and accessible than those delivered by formal education providers which do not easily accommodate pre-entry level students with mixed abilities, and that do not provide space for women to help and support each other and build social solidarity with each other. Women also reported that they were unable to attend such classes where their husbands or families restricted them from associating with men.

The women's project provided a range of women-only services that supported the women to develop their knowledge and social capital, as well as to reflect on intersectional and institutional oppressions experienced in their personal lives and in their access to services. These intersectional oppressions took the form of gendered cultural traditions, barriers to accessing complex services and structures, and prejudice from wider society based on their gender, religion, cultures and ethnicities. Workshops that centred on specific issues, and the development of social solidarity with each other, enabled the women to become more aware of inequalities they and other women face and to feel able to respond to or overcome these barriers. This was particularly the case for those regular attendees who became volunteers and staff or who expressed a desire to help change things for their children or other women in the future. This is most explicit in the women's narratives in year three of the project (see Chapter 7) with Firouzeh's desire to create a men's project because 'we need to change *their* minds... so the limits for the women can go' a strong example of the women's growing awareness of inequalities and desire to effect change for other women.

GRASSROOTS PRACTICE AND POSSIBLE LIMITS TO INTEGRATION

The women's project was a safe and accessible space due to the presence of insider-practitioners who understood the women's lives, challenges and cultures. The grassroots nature of the project, in that it was created and led by those from refugee backgrounds themselves, meant that it was able to be culturally relatable and needs-sensitive. The need for the sense of 'safety' this creates is a key principle of trauma-informed practice (SAMHSA, 2014), especially where other services and institutions have exacerbated experiences of trauma and prejudice.

However, we have also discussed whether the provision of such safe spaces, where women engage with others they share characteristics with, presents some limitations to facilitating their integration. This dilemma was captured by project worker, Sarah, in year three who stated that 'There's a balance that's hard to strike between supporting women to celebrate their own culture and explore wider cultures'. We have drawn on Bright, Thompson, Hart, and Hayden's (2018) notion of 'inclusion within' to justify the need for such safe spaces before broader inclusion and integration can be developed for marginalised groups. Finding this balance is part of the two-way integration process adopted by the project, where the women's lives, cultures and identities should not need to be sacrificed in order to integrate into their new society.

INCORPORATING A BALANCED MODEL THAT RESPONDS TO NEEDS AND BUILDS ON ASSETS

Whilst asset-focused interventions have become dominant in community development, there is a danger that a deliberate focus away from the needs of vulnerable groups may cement rather than tackle inequalities, and collude with a political and neoliberal agenda that promotes individualism and austerity (MacLeod & Emejulu, 2014). We have argued it is necessary to develop more interventions that respond to the needs of marginalised groups before building on their strengths to address them.

It is important such needs-sensitive interventions are bottom-up rather than top-down, and that needs and responses are defined through engagement with the communities being served. The women's project demonstrated such an approach where a focus on the need for particular knowledge and skills was later able to shift towards a focus on assets and peer empowerment, where women led workshops and became staff and volunteers. Such empowerment needed them to have developed the required knowledge capital, skills and resources as well as to have built social solidarity with each other. This was a long-term process where, in year one of the project, women started bringing food to share and raising topics for workshops, in year two they began to deliver workshops to their peers, and by year three, women who had engaged long-term were volunteers and staff at the project. The move from needs to assets was observed as women began to take more leadership over workshops and wider delivery of the project, and expressed support for and solidarity with each other. This can be seen across the qualitative data and is captured in the 'journey of change' (see Fig. 2 in Chapter 7). This builds on other research (as explored in Chapter 4) which found combined approaches, focused on both assets and needs, can be more effective, as well as that a focus on needs has more short-term impact with a focus on assets having longer-term impacts (Hebert-Beirne et al., 2018; Nel, 2018).

Other, less marginalised, groups with more social and knowledge capital may be able to develop peer empowerment activities from the outset. For example, as in Eidoo's (2016) research (discussed in Chapter 4) which found young Muslim women in Canada were developing their own community spaces in which they took refuge from Islamophobia, racism and cultural patriarchal restrictions, and were developing their own forms of learning, community and citizenship. For the most marginalised and isolated groups, the ground work involves responding to their needs over time and a longer-term process of drawing on their strengths and assets to facilitate peer empowerment. However, as a grassroots organisation, the staff delivering the women's project from the start were, to an extent, peers and insiders with the women who attended.

A MODEL OF LONG-TERM EMPOWERMENT

The research with the women's project demonstrates that empowerment is a long-term process for the most isolated and marginalised groups. Sustainable change takes significant time to achieve and, as outlined above, involves starting with a focus on needs before building on assets, for women who are almost completely isolated. Fig. 3 represents the process of empowerment that occurs over time, moving from aspirational to sustainable change, as drawn out in Chapters 5 to 7.

From their starting point of isolation and marginalisation, we observed the women in our research becoming more aspirational as they accessed support from the women's project. Through the project they were supported to enter the aspirational empowerment stage as they began to form long-term goals for their lives as well as becoming more aware of the barriers they (and other women) faced to their empowerment and integration. From there, we observed in year two of the project, small changes being manifested in their lives as they set and met objectives towards their long-term goals, and gained a broader awareness of inequalities in the tangible empowerment stage, supported by action planning, mentoring and topical workshops.

In the third year of the project we observed that larger changes were manifested in the women's lives and even some of their long-term goals were being met. In some of the narratives in Chapter 7, it appeared these changes were becoming sustainable and that further change would be possible without

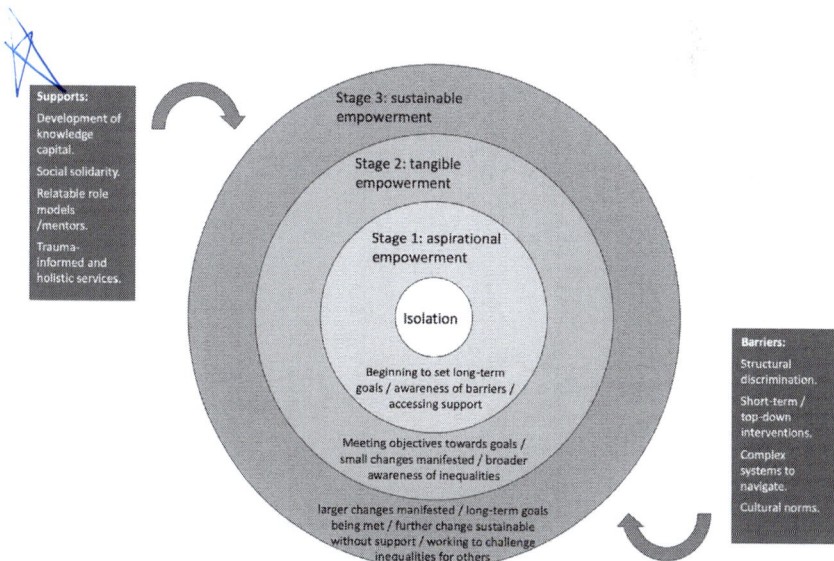

Fig. 3. Model of Long-Term Empowerment for Marginalised Groups.

support. In their roles as volunteers and staff, they were also beginning to work to challenge inequalities for others, as in Firouzeh's plan to set up a men's project to educate them to remove the limitations placed on women. Such examples demonstrate women entering the sustainable empowerment stage. This is not to suggest that the process takes three full years (nor that it is in all cases linear and progressive through the stages) as attendance was often fluctuating with new groups coming and going throughout the three years. However, it is the women who engaged long-term (generally for a year or more) who saw the most substantial changes to their lives.

Whilst this model of long-term empowerment is based on our research with migrant and refugee women, it could be applied to other isolated groups. The supports and barriers may vary between groups and further research is needed to test applicability beyond our case study. Nevertheless, the diagram illustrates how marginalised groups might move through the stages of empowerment we observed in our research over time.

The illustration in Fig. 3 includes some of the supports and barriers that emerged in our research. These are not exhaustive lists and may vary between groups and communities. As shown in the diagram, some of the supports that emerged in our study include the development of knowledge capital, social solidarity, access to relatable role models and mentors, facilitated through the provision of trauma-informed and holistic support services. Some of the barriers to empowerment identified throughout the preceding chapters include structural discrimination, short-term and top-down interventions, complex systems to navigate, and cultural and gender norms that restricted empowerment. Restrictions to empowerment can be exercised from the inside and outside for minority cultural, religious and/or racialized communities, through cultural limitations from the inside or 'othering' by society from the outside. More widely, these restrictions might also extend to other 'cultures' and 'norms' that exist for other marginalised groups, including class culture, for example, as one element of the intersectional identities of marginalised groups.

Supporting marginalised groups to overcome barriers and reach the sustainable empowerment stage requires long-term engagement rather than short-term programmes. In the case of the women's project, this was achieved through a holistic approach that brought otherwise disparate and patchy service provision together. Recognising internal and external barriers to integration for marginalised communities requires integration policy and practice to frame integration as a two-way process, in order to break down structural barriers and realise the importance of cultural accessibility and of not completely erasing cultural identities. Holistic integration services should include responses to mental health and trauma alongside a practical focus on skills and knowledge needed for integration such as learning English and understanding systems and services. Our research suggests policy and practice needs to recognise the range of diverse and varied integration outcomes rather than focusing only on top-down narrow hard outcomes. For example, a narrow focus on engagement with employment may be misdirected, where it is not the desired or necessary outcome for many migrant women, whereas softer but significant outcomes may be disregarded.

The long-term process of empowerment we observed in the women's project was supported by relationships between women and with staff. For many of the women, having a social network outside of their families was a new experience, as demonstrated by their narratives in Chapters 5 and 6. This suggests that any measures of empowerment and integration need to consider the distance travelled. For marginalised refugee and migrant women, the level of isolation at the point of engagement is significant. This meant that some of them did not travel the full journey of change (Fig. 2 in Chapter 7) or reach the sustainable empowerment stage (Fig. 3) even with long-term engagement. Such models need to not be fixed but viewed as reflexive and adaptable tools for particular groups and their starting points, needs, assets and challenges. As already highlighted, challenges to embedding long-term empowerment processes within broader policy and practice include the drive for short-term narrowly measured outcomes and, as such, the precarity of funding for long-term initiatives.

MENTAL HEALTH AND TRAUMA

The women's empowerment was supported by the holistic and intersectional model adopted by the women's project. Within such a model, recognition of trauma should not be reserved for specific mental health interventions. All work with migrant and refugee groups should be trauma-informed whether it is delivery of English classes, practical workshops, individual or group support, or specific mental health interventions. Whilst the women in our research have shown great resilience, as demonstrated in their narratives throughout this book, they have also experienced many traumas, and these require a trauma-informed approach. A focus on building resilience has been criticised as a neoliberal expression of community work practice (Mayo, 2021; Ní Charraighe, 2019). The need for a trauma-informed approach supports our argument that a focus on recognising needs and on overcoming challenges is required for community development with the most marginalised (and, indeed, traumatised) groups as well as building on their assets and potential.

The principles of trauma-informed practice (such as safety, peer support, choice and voice, empowerment, and recognition of cultural, gender and other issues) can be observed in the practice of the women's project over the three years (SAMHSA, 2014). For example, feeling safe emerged as a key theme in year two (see Chapter 6), peer support was embedded and grew throughout the three years, and within the overall aim of empowering the women. Additionally, several of these principles overlap with the key principles of community development more broadly, particularly with the values of empowerment, collaboration and challenging discrimination (CLD Standards Council, 2021; ESB, 2015).

The women also needed some specific mental health support and were not generally accessing this outside of the women's project – with such interventions found to be often unrepresentative and unrelatable for minority groups (Nurein & Iqbal, 2021). The analysis of the 'body and mind' workshops, as well as the broader literature, in Chapter 8 suggests creative methods can contribute to a therapeutic approach that works for groups and individuals with multiple traumas and low levels of English, affecting their ability to express their experiences and feelings. However, the two 'body and mind' workshops were an ad hoc introduction to such an approach and there is arguably a need for more consistent and long-term therapeutic support. Aminah, one of the project workers interviewed in year three recognised that over time 'the women have become more open to talking about personal and sensitive issues and trauma'. However, the provision of specialist mental health services for migrant and refugee groups, and indeed community mental health services more broadly, is impacted by lack of statutory funding, and where funding is available, it does not often support long-term interventions. In particular, there is a lack of tailored mental health support for migrant and refugee women that recognises and responds to their intersectional identities and traumas (Nurein & Iqbal, 2021).

PRECARIOUS PRACTICE

Community work projects such as the women's project face a significant level of precariousness in their delivery of holistic and long-term support services to marginalised communities. In the case of the women's project, precarity of funding which meant a reliance on volunteers, and on parts of the work being delivered 'in kind' by the charity, led to disruption and inconsistency at times. These inconsistencies affected the location and frequency of provision, as well as staff changes meaning disruption to the staff and volunteers who were building relationships with the women.

Such precarities lead to patchiness and inequity of provision available to migrant and refugee women, as well as other marginalised groups, and often a reliance on the voluntary and community sector to provide essential support. Within this, grant funding is often focused on new projects rather than continued support, and usually reflects the same neoliberal focus on short-termism and hard outcomes that beleaguers the statutory sector. When our research finished, for example, the future of the women's project was unclear with its three years of grant funding also coming to an end. Arguably, austerity localism is failing migrant and refugee women and other marginalised groups.

Our research demonstrates that for the most marginalised migrant and refugee groups, and particularly for women who can be very isolated, empowerment and integration are long-term processes that require significant support to address the need for knowledge capital, social solidarity, English language learning and mental health services. These needs require a level of response before sustainable asset-focused empowerment can be facilitated. As such, there is a need for a considered and nuanced policy commitment and substantial funding for long-term support for refugee and migrant women, and indeed for other marginalised groups. Such support needs to involve grassroots practitioners and organisations in both policy development and delivery in order that it remains bottom-up, culturally sensitive, anti-discriminatory and accessible.

RESEARCH IMPLICATIONS

In addition to the policy and practice implications outlined above, some implications for research with migrant and refugee women also emerge from the study of the women's project. Perhaps most crucially, the importance of insiders in research was explored in Chapter 2. As well as insiders being important in practice, insider-researchers are key to gaining trust in research with vulnerable groups such as migrant and refugee women. However, we also explored the fluidity of researcher positionalities as insiders and outsiders in Chapter 2, with the researcher role in itself setting the researcher, to an extent, apart (Narayen, 1993). Differences in role, status and authority impact on the researcher's level of insider status. Additionally, external researchers also face a level of fluidity over how far they are an insider or outsider with their participants, through characteristics such as gender, parental status, heritage and culture. As such, it is important to understand our own intersectional identities as researchers and how these act on the research. These intersectional identities define our status as insiders and outsiders in different ways at different times, in how they overlap (or not) with the identities of the research participants. Navigating this fluidity of status and being aware of its impact requires reflexivity to be built into the research approach.

In Chapter 8, we highlighted the potential for the use of creative methods in research with migrant and refugee groups, especially where there are language barriers. There is also clear potential to explore emotions and journeys associated with trauma through arts-based methods, where speaking may alone may be a more challenging way to express such experiences. While we did not use such methods substantially in this study, the analysis of the 'body and mind' workshops demonstrates how important themes can emerge through such creativity of expression.

There is a need for more bottom-up research and policy that understands the experiences of migrant and refugee women as well as which interventions are effective. The study of the women's project in this book highlights that research and evaluation (and indeed, also practice) with refugee and migrant women (as well as other marginalised groups) needs to be reflexive and responsive. In particular, projects should not be focused on fixed and narrow markers of integration but open to these being defined by participants through the research and evaluation processes. In the case of the women's project, a range of soft outcomes such as those relating to confidence, wellbeing and social solidarity, emerge from the data presented in Chapters 5 to 7. Crucially, this means a focus on qualitative methods to allow the voices and narratives of participants to be central to research findings, and not a dominance of quantitative measures. Within this qualitative approach, the use of ethnographic and longitudinal methods in our study allowed for data to be gathered with the women over time. This meant we could explore long-term processes of empowerment and change, often missed in how policy and practice are measured and evaluated. The women's project case study demonstrates that for both research and practice, the most meaningful change is curated and captured over time.

Overall, the case study has implications for policy, practice and for meaningful research with migrant and refugee women. These implications have relevance beyond the UK-based case study because of the current global focus on issues surrounding refugees and migration. Our research offers a challenge to policy and practice informed by problematic discourses such as populism and prejudice and argues instead for the need to challenge these stigmatising discourses and promote grassroots practice with refugee and migrant populations, and other marginalised groups, that meets their needs and builds on their strengths.

BIBLIOGRAPHY

Abbas, T., & Awan, I. (2015). Limits of UK counterterrorism policy and its implications for Islamophobia. *International Journal for Crime, Justice & Social Democracy*, 4(3), 16–29. doi:10.5204/ijcjsd.v4i3.241

Ahmed, S. (2015). The voices of young British Muslims: Identity, belonging and citizenship. In M. K. Smith, N. Stanton, & T. Wylie (Eds.), *Youth work and faith: Debates, delights and dilemmas* (pp. 37–51). Lyme Regis: Russell House.

Ali, S. (2015). *British Muslims in numbers*. Retrieved from http://www.mcb.org.uk/wp-content/uploads/2015/02/MCBCensusReport_2015.pdf

American Psychiatric Association. (2013). *Diagnostic and statistical manual of mental disorders* (5th ed.). Washington, DC: APA.

Anjum, S., McVittie, C., & McKinlay, A. (2018). It is not quite cricket: Muslim immigrants' accounts of integration into UK society. *European Journal of Social Psychology*, 48(1), 1–14. doi:10.1002/ejsp.2280

Anthias, F. (2012). Transnational mobilities, migration research and intersectionality: Towards a translocational frame. *Nordic Journal of Migration Research*, 2(2), 102–110. doi:10.2478/v10202-011-0032-y

Bariso, E. U. (2008). Factors affecting participation in adult education: A case study of participation in Hackney and Waltham Forest, London. *Studies in the Education of Adults*, 40(1), 110–124. doi:10.1080/02660830.2008.11661559

Belton, B. (2009). *Developing critical youth work theory*. Rotterdam: Sense.

Belton, B. (2017). Colonised youth. *Youth & Policy*. Retrieved from https://www.youthandpolicy.org/articles/colonised-youth/

Berger, R. (2015). Now I see it, now I don't: Researcher's position and reflexivity in qualitative research. *Qualitative Research*, 15(2), 219–234. doi:10.1177/1468794112468475

Berner, E., & Phillips, B. (2005). Left to their own devices? Community self-help between alternative development and neo-liberalism. *Community Development Journal*, 40(1), 17–29. doi:10.1093/cdj/bsi003

Berry, J. (2005). Acculturation: Living successfully in two cultures. *International Journal of Intercultural Relations*, *29*(6), 697–712. doi:10.1016/j.ijintrel.2005.07.013

Botterill, K. (2015). We don't see things as they are, we see things as we are: Questioning the 'outsider' in Polish migration research. *Qualitative Sozialforschung/Forum for Qualitative Social Research*, *16*(2). doi:10.17169/fqs-16.2.2331

Bourdieu, P. (1996). Understanding. *Theory, Culture and Society*, *13*(2), 17–37. doi:10.1177/026327696013002002

Bradbury-Jones, C. (2007). Enhancing rigor in qualitative health research: Exploring subjectivity through Peshkin's I's. *Journal of Advanced Nursing*, *59*(3), 290–298. doi:10.1111/j.1365-2648.2007.04306.x

Brennan, R., Bush, M., Trickey, D., Levene, C., & Watson, J. (2019). *Adversity and trauma-informed practice: A short guide for professionals working on the frontline*. London: YoungMinds.

Bright, G., Thompson, N., Hart, P., & Hayden, B. (2018). Faith-based youth work: Education, engagement and ethics. In P. Alldred, F. Cullen, K. Edwards, & D. Fusco (Eds.), *Sage handbook of youth work practice* (pp. 197–212). London: Sage.

Callaghan, K. (1998). In limbo, movement psychotherapy with refugees and asylum seekers. In D. Dokter (Ed.), *Arts therapists, refugees and migrants: Reaching across borders* (pp. 25–39). London: Jessica Kingsley Publishers.

Casey, L. (2016). *The Casey Review: A review into opportunity and integration*. London: Department for Communities and Local Government.

Change Institute. (2009). *The Afghan Muslim community in England: Understanding Muslim ethnic communities*. London: Change Institute.

Cheung, S., & Phillimore, J. (2017). Gender and refugee integration: A quantitative analysis of integration and social policy outcomes. *Journal of Social Policy*, *46*(2), 211–230. doi:10.1017/S0047279416000775

CLD Standards Council Scotland. (2021). Values of CLD. Retrieved from https://cldstandardscouncil.org.uk/resources/values-of-cld/

Cloke, P., Crang, P., & Goodwin, M. (2005). *Introducing human geographies*. London: Hodder Arnold.

Collyer, M., Morrice, L., Tip, L., Brown, R., & Odermatt, E. (2018). *A long-term commitment: Integration of resettled refugees in the UK*. Brighton: University of Sussex. Retrieved from https://www.sussex.ac.uk/webteam/gateway/file.php?name=4375-resettled-refugees-report-web.pdf&site=252

Conner, M. K. (2020). *A proposed music therapy protocol for trauma-informed, culturally aware practice with migrants at the US-Mexico border.* Unpublished Masters Thesis, Lesley University, Cambridge, MA. Retrieved from https://digitalcommons.lesley.edu/expressive_theses/253

Cooke, M., & Simpson, J. (2009). Challenging agendas in ESOL: Skills, employability and social cohesion. *Language Issues, 20*(1), 19–30.

Coppock, V., & McGovern, M. (2014). Dangerous minds? Deconstructing counter-terrorism discourse, radicalisation and the 'psychological vulnerability' of Muslim children and young people in Britain. *Children & Society, 28*(3), 242–256. doi:10.1111/chso.12060

Cree, V. E. (2010). *Sociology for social workers and probation officers.* London: Routledge.

Crenshaw, K. (1989). Demarginalizing the intersection of race and sex: A black feminist critique of antidiscrimination doctrine, feminist theory and antiracist politics. *University of Chicago Legal Forum, 8*, 139–168. Retrieved from https://chicagounbound.uchicago.edu/uclf/vol1989/iss1/8

Denscombe, M. (2007). *The good research guide* (3rd ed.). Maidenhead: Open University Press.

DfES. (2003). *Working with refugees and asylum seekers: Support materials for ESOL providers.* London: Department for Education and Skills. Retrieved from https://esol.excellencegateway.org.uk/vocabulary/EGresourcetype/Effective%20practice%20example

Dimitriadou, A. (2004). The formation of social capital for refugee students: An exploration of ESOL settings in two further education colleges. *Educate, 4*(1), 31–45. Retrieved from http://www.educatejournal.org/index.php/educate/article/view/78

Dokter, D. (Ed.). (1998). *Arts therapists, refugees and migrants: Reaching across borders.* London: Jessica Kingsley Publishers.

Doyle, L., & O'Toole, G. (2013). *A lot to learn: Refugees, asylum seekers and post-16 learning.* London: Refugee Council. Retrieved from https://www.refugeecouncil.org.uk/information/resources/a-lot-to-learn/

Drake, P. (2010). Grasping at methodological understanding: A cautionary tale from insider research. *International Journal of Research and Method in Education, 33*(1), 85–99. doi:10.1080/17437271003597592

Eidoo, S. (2016). Pedagogies of Muslim feminisms: Reflections on faith, space and citizenship. *Gender and Education*, *30*(4), 513–529. doi:10.1080/09540253.2016.1225016

ESB. (2015). ESB NOS 2015 outline. Retrieved from http://www.esbendorsement.org.uk/index.php/nos-2015-guidance-from-esb/download?path=ESB%2BNOS%2B2015%2BOutline%2BWebsite.pdf

European Union External Action. (2017). Joint way forward on migration issues between Afghanistan and the EU. Retrieved from https://eeas.europa.eu/sites/eeas/files/eu_afghanistan_joint_way_forward_on_migration_issues.pdf

Fancourt, D., Warran, K., & Aughterson, H. (2020). *Evidence summary for policy: The role of arts in improving health and wellbeing.* London: Department for Digital, Culture, Media & Sport.

Featherstone, D., Ince, A., MacKinnon, D., Strauss, K., & Cumbers, A. (2012). Progressive localism and the construction of political alternatives. *Transactions of the Institute of British Geographers*, *37*, 177–182. doi:10.1111/j.1475-5661.2011.00493.x

Finefter-Rosenbluh, I. (2017). Incorporating perspective taking in reflexivity. *International Journal of Qualitative Methods*, *16*, 1–11. doi:10.1177/1609406917703539

Fitzsimons, A., Hope, M., Cooper, C., & Russell, K. (2011). *Empowerment and participation in youth work.* Exeter: Learning Matters.

Foucault, M. (1970). *The order of things: An archaeology of the human sciences.* London: Routledge.

García-Medrano, S., & Panhofer, H. (2020). Improving migrant well-being: Spontaneous movement as a way to increase the creativity, spontaneity and welfare of migrants in Glasgow. *Body, Movement and Dance in Psychotherapy*, *15*(3), 189–203. doi:10.1080/17432979.2020.1767208

Gateley, D. (2015). A policy of vulnerability or agency? Refugee young people's opportunities in accessing further and higher education in the UK. *Compare: A Journal of Comparative and International Education*, *45*(1), 26–46. doi:10.1080/03057925.2013.841030

Giusta, M. D., & Kambhampati, U. (2006). Women migrant workers in the UK: Social capital, well-being and integration. *Journal of International Development*, *18*(6), 819–833. doi:10.1002/jid.1316

Goodman, R. D., Vesely, C. K., Letiecq, B., & Cleavelant, C. L. (2017). Trauma and resilience among refugee and undocumented women. *Journal of Counselling and Development*, *95*(3), 309–321. doi:10.1002/jcad.12145

Goodson, L., & Phillimore, J. (2010). A community research methodology: Working with new migrants to develop a policy related evidence base. *Social Policy and Society*, *9*(4), 489–501. doi:10.1017/S1474746410000217

Governance Now. (2016). Learn English or face deportation, UK PM tells migrant Muslim women. Retrieved from https://www.governancenow.com/news/regular-story/learn-english-or-face-deportation-uk-pm-tells-migrant-muslim-women. Accessed on May 1, 2020.

Greenfields, M., & Ryder, A. (2012). Research with and for Gypsies, Roma and Travellers: Combining policy, practice and community in action research. In J. Richardson & A. Ryder (Eds.), *Gypsies and travellers: Empowerment and inclusion in British society* (pp. 15–168). Bristol: Policy Press.

Griffith, A. I. (1998). Insider/outsider: Epistemological privilege and mothering work. *Human Studies*, *21*, 361–376. doi:10.1023/A:1005421211078

Guillemin, M., & Gillam, L. (2004). Ethics, reflexivity and 'ethically important moments' in research. *Qualitative Inquiry*, *10*(2), 261–280. doi:10.1177/1077800403262360

Hall, S. (1995). Negotiating Caribbean identities. *New Left Review*, *1*(209), 3–14. Retrieved from https://newleftreview.org/issues/i209

Hanania, A. (2018). A proposal for culturally informed art therapy with refugee women: The potential for trauma expression through embroidery. *Canadian Art Therapy Association Journal*, *31*(1), 33–42. doi:10.1080/08322473.2017.1378516

Harinen, P. M., Honkasalo, M. V., Ronkainen, J. K., & Suurpaa, L. E. (2012). Multiculturalism and young people's leisure spaces in Finland: Perspectives of multicultural youth. *Leisure Studies*, *31*, 177–191. doi:10.1080/08322473.2017.1378516

Haverig, A. (2013). Managing integration: German and British policy responses to the 'threat from within' post-2001. *Journal of International Migration and Integration*, *14*(2), 345–362. doi:10.1007/s12134-012-0245-5

Hebert-Beirne, J., Hernandez, S., Felner, J., Schwiesow, J., Mayer, A., Rak, K., ... Kennelly, J. (2018). Using community-driven, participatory qualitative inquiry to discern nuanced community health needs and assets of Chicago's La

Villita, a Mexican immigrant neighborhood. *Journal of Community Health*, *43*(4), 775–786. doi:10.1007/s10900-018-0484-2

Higton, J., Sandhu, J., Stutz, A., Patel, R., Choudhoury, A., & Richards, S. (2019). *English for speakers of other languages: Access and progression*. London: Department for Education.

Home Office. (2015). *Counter extremism strategy*. London: Crown Copyright.

Home Office. (2021). National statistics: How many people do we grant asylum or protection to? Retrieved from https://www.gov.uk/government/statistics/immigration-statistics-year-ending-june-2021/how-many-people-do-we-grant-asylum-or-protection-to

Horsburgh, D. (2003). Evaluation of qualitative research. *Journal of Clinical Nursing*, *12*(2), 307–312. doi:10.1046/j.1365-2702.2003.00683.x

Horváth, Z. E., Szakács, A., & Szakács, Z. (2018). Insider research on diversity and inclusion: Methodological considerations. *Mednarodno Inovativno Poslovanje*, *10*(1), 1–11. doi:10.32015/JIMB/2018-10-1-3

IDeA. (2010). *A glass half full: How an asset approach can improve community health and wellbeing*. London: Improvement and Development Agency; Local Government Association.

International Rescue Committee. (2020). Gender equality: Women's rights are advancing—But are refugees being left behind? Retrieved from https://www.rescue-uk.org/article/womens-rights-are-advancing-are-refugees-being-left-behind

Israel, B. A., Eng, E., Schulz, A. J., & Parker, E. A. (Eds.). (2005). *Methods in community-based participatory research for health*. San Francisco, CA: Jossey-Bass.

Jason, L., & Glenwick, D. (Eds.). (2016). *Approaches to community-based research: Qualitative, quantitative and mixed methods*. Oxford: Oxford University Press.

Jimerson, D. (2017). *(Re)painting self: Art therapy and ontological security in refugee children*. Capstone Projects and Master's Theses (p. 344). Retrieved from https://digitalcommons.csumb.edu/caps_thes_all/344/

Klenk, H. (2017). An alternative understanding of education and empowerment: Local-level perspectives of refugee social integration in the United Kingdom. *European Education*, *49*, 166–183. doi:10.1080/10564934.2017.1341290

Kloos, B., Hill, J., Thomas, E., Wandersman, A., Elias, M. J., & Dalton, J. H. (2012). *Community psychology.* Belmont, CA: Cengage Learning.

Kortmann, M. (2015). Asking those concerned: How Muslim migrant organisations define integration. A German-Dutch comparison. *Journal of International Migration and Integration, 16*(4), 1057–1080. doi:10.1007/s12134-014-0387-8

Lipson, J. G., & Meleis, A. I. (1989). Methodological issues in research with immigrants. *Medical Anthropology, 12*(1), 103–115. doi:10.1080/01459740.1989.9966014

Lodrick, Z. (2007). Psychological trauma–what every trauma worker should know. *The British Journal of Psychotherapy Integration, 4*(2), 18–28. Retrieved from http://www.ukapi.uk/

Mackey, L. (2019). *North west ESOL co-ordination report April 2018 - March 2019.* Manchester: Northwest Regional Strategic Migration Partnership.

MacLeod, M. A., & Emejulu, A. (2014). Neoliberalism with a community face? A critical analysis of asset-based community development in Scotland. *Journal of Community Practice, 22*(4), 430–450. doi:10.1080/10705422.2014.959147

Mandaville, P. (2009). Muslim transnational identity and state responses in Europe and the UK after 9/11: Political community, ideology and authority. *Journal of Ethnic and Migration Studies, 35*(3), 491–506. doi:10.1080/13691830802704681

Masten, A., & Narayan, A. (2012). Child development in the context of disaster, war, and terrorism: Pathways of risk and resilience. *Annual Review of Psychology, 63*, 227–257. doi:10.1146/annurev-psych-120710-100356

Maynes, M. J., Pierce, J. L., & Laslett, B. (2008). *Telling stories.* New York, NY: Cornell University Press.

Mayo, M. (2017). *Changing communities: Stories of migration, displacement and solidarities.* Bristol: Policy Press.

Mayo, M. (2021). The importance of community-based learning. In H. Tam (Ed.), *Tomorrow's communities* (pp. 111–126). Bristol: Policy Press.

McKnight, J., & Kretzmann, J. (2012). Mapping community capacity. In M. Minkler (Ed.), *Community organizing and community building for health and welfare* (3rd ed., pp. 171–186). New Brunswick, NJ: Rutgers University Press.

McManus, S., Bebbington, P., Jenkins, R., & Brugha, T. (Eds.). (2016). *Mental health and well-being in England: The adult psychiatric morbidity survey 2014.* Leeds: NHS Digital. Retrieved from https://assets.publishing.

service.gov.uk/government/uploads/system/uploads/attachment_data/file/
556596/apms-2014-full-rpt.pdf

Mercer, J. (2007). The challenges of insider research in educational
institutions: Wielding a double-edged sword and resolving delicate dilemmas.
Oxford Review of Education, *33*(1), 1–17. doi:10.1080/03054980601094651

Merton, R. K. (1972). Insiders and outsiders: A chapter in the sociology of
knowledge. *American Journal of Sociology*, *78*(1), 9–47. doi:10.1086/225294

Minkler, M. (2005). Community-based research partnerships: Challenges and
opportunities. *Journal of Urban Health*, *82*(2 Suppl), ii3–ii12. doi:10.1093/
jurban/jti034

Mirza, H. (2010). 'Walking on eggshells': Multiculturalism, gender and
domestic violence. In M. Robb & R. Thomson (Eds.), *Critical practice with
children and young people* (pp. 43–58). Bristol: Policy Press.

Missingham, B. (2017). Asset-based learning and the pedagogy of community
development. *Community Development Journal*, *48*(3), 339–350. doi:10.
1080/15575330.2017.1291528

Morrice, L., Tip, L., Collyer, M., & Brown, R. (2019). You can't have a good
integration when you don't have a good communication: English-language
learning among resettled refugees in England. *Journal of Refugee Studies*,
34(1), 681–699. doi:10.1093/jrs/fez023

Mulvey, G. (2009). *Refugee and asylum seeker research in Scotland: A
literature review*. Glasgow: Scottish Refugee Council.

Narayan, K. (1993). How native is a 'native' anthropologist? *American
Anthropologist*, *95*(3), 671–686. doi:10.1525/aa.1993.95.3.02a00070

Neale, B., & Flowerdew, J. (2003). Time texture and childhood: The contours
of qualitative longitudinal research. *International Journal of Social Research
Methodology: Theory and Practice*, *6*(3), 189–199. doi:10.1080/
1364557032000091798

Nel, H. (2018). A comparison between the asset-oriented and needs-based
community development approaches in terms of systems changes. *Practice*,
30(1), 33–52. doi:10.1080/09503153.2017.1360474

Nellums, L., Rustage, K., Hargreaves, S., Friedland, J., Miller, A., & Hiam, L.
(2018). *Access to healthcare for people seeking and refused asylum in Great
Britain: A review of evidence*. London: Equality and Human Rights
Commission Research Report Series.

Nellums, L., Rustage, K., Hargreaves, S., Friedland, J., Miller, A., Hiam, L., & Le Deaut, D. (2018). *The lived experiences of access to healthcare for people seeking and refused asylum*. London: Equality and Human Rights Commission Research Report Series.

Ní Charraighe, A. (2019). Re/membering resilience–a reflection on resilience and youth work. *Youth & Policy*. Retrieved from https://www.youthandpolicy.org/articles/re-membering-resilience/

Nijhowne, D., & Oates, L. (2008). *Living with violence: A national report on domestic abuse in Afghanistan*. Washington, DC: Global Rights, Partners for Justice.

Nurein, A., & Iqbal, H. (2021). Identifying a space for young Black Muslim women in Contemporary Britain. *Ethnicities*, 21(3), 433–453. doi:10.1177/14687968211001899

NUS. (2018). The experience of Muslim students in 2017–2018. Retrieved from https://www.nusconnect.org.uk/resources/the-experience-of-muslim-students-in-2017-18

O'Donnell, A. W., Stuart, J., & O'Donnell, K. J. (2020). The long term financial and psychological resettlement outcomes of pre-migration trauma and post-settlement difficulties in resettled refugees. *Social Science & Medicine*, 262(113246). doi:10.1016/j.socscimed.2020.113246

OECD. (2018). *Working together for local integration of migrants and refugees*. OECD Regional Development Studies. Paris: OECD Publishing. doi: 10.1787/9789264085350-en

Papadopoulos, R. K. (2021). *Involuntary dislocation: Home, trauma, resilience and adversity-activated development*. London: Routledge.

Phillimore, J., Ergun, E., Goodson, L., & Hennessy, D. (2007). *Now I do it for myself: Refugees and ESOL*. New York, NY: Joseph Rowntree Foundation. Retrieved from http://www.bncn.org.uk/partnerships/community-research/

Philo, G., Briant, E., & Donald, P. (2013). *Bad news for refugees*. London: Pluto Press.

Pillow, W. S. (2003). Confession, catharsis, or cure? Rethinking the uses of reflexivity as methodological power in qualitative research. *International Journal of Qualitative Studies in Education*, 16(2), 175–196. doi:10.1080/0951839032000060635

Pollard, T., & Howard, N. (2021). Mental healthcare for asylum-seekers and refugees residing in the United Kingdom: A scoping review of policies, barriers, and enablers. *International Journal of Mental Health Systems*, *15*(60). doi:10.1186/s13033-021-00473-z

Priebe, S., & El-Nagib, R. (2016). *Public health aspects of mental health among migrants and refugees: A review of the evidence on mental health care for refugees, asylum seekers and irregular migrants in the WHO European region*. Geneva: World Health Organization.

Priebe, S., & Giacco, D. (2018). *Mental health promotion and mental health care in refugees and migrants: Technical guidance*. Geneva: World Health Organisation. Retrieved from https://www.euro.who.int/__data/assets/pdf_file/0004/386563/mental-health-eng.pdf

Public Health England. (2019). Advice and guidance on the health needs of migrant patients for healthcare practitioners. Retrieved from https://www.gov.uk/guidance/mental-health-migrant-health-guide

Refugee Action. (2016). Facts about refugees: Claiming asylum is a human right. Retrieved from https://www.refugee-action.org.uk/about/facts-about-refugees/#:~:text=The%20definition%20of%20an%20asylum,or%20a%20British%20citizen%20would

Refugee Action. (2017a). *Safe but alone: The role of English language in allowing refugees to overcome loneliness*. London: Refugee Action.

Refugee Action. (2017b). *Locked out of learning: A snapshot of ESOL provision in England*. London: Refugee Action. Retrieved from https://www.refugee-action.org.uk/resource/locked-learning-snapshot-esol-provision-england/

Refugee Action. (2018). *Waiting in the dark: How the asylum system dehumanises, disempowers and damages*. London: Refugee Action. Retrieved from https://www.refugee-action.org.uk/wp-content/uploads/2018/05/Waiting-in-the-Dark-Report.pdf

Refugee Council. (2021a). *Asylum statistics annual trends May 2021*. London: Refugee Council.

Refugee Council. (2021b). Asylum backlog reaches a record high, including over 3,000 Afghans. Retrieved from https://www.refugeecouncil.org.uk/latest/news/asylum-backlog-reaches-a-record-high-including-over-3000-afghans/

Refugee Support Network. (2012). *'I just want to study': Access to higher education for young refugees and asylum seekers*. London: Refugee Support Network.

Rose, G. (1997). Situating knowledges: Positionality, reflexivities and other tactics. *Progress in Human Geography*, *21*(3), 305–320. doi:10.1191/030913297673302122

Rostami-Povey, E. (2007). Afghan refugees in Iran, Pakistan, the U.K., and the U.S. and life after return: A comparative gender analysis. *Iranian Studies*, *40*(2), 241-261. doi:10.1080/00210860701269576

Rova, M., Burrell, C., & Cohen, M. (2020). Existing in-between two worlds: Supporting asylum seeking women living in temporary accommodation through a creative movement and art intervention. *Body, Movement and Dance in Psychotherapy*, *15*(3), 204–218. doi:10.1080/17432979.2020.1772370

Ryan, L. (2015). 'Inside' and 'outside' of what or where? Researching migration through multi-positionalities. *Forum Qualitative Sozialforschung/Forum for Qualitative Social Research*, *16*(2). doi:10.17169/fqs-16.2.2333

Sadan, E. (2004). *Empowerment and community practice (ebook)*. Retrieved from http://www.mpow.org/

Salvo, T., & de C Williams, A. C. (2017). 'If I speak English, what am I? I am full man, me': Emotional impact and barriers for refugees and asylum seekers learning English. *Transcultural Psychiatry*, *54*(5/6), 733–755. doi:10.1177/1363461517746315

SAMHSA. (2014). *SAMHSA's concept of trauma and guidance for a trauma-informed approach*. Rockville, MD: Substance Abuse and Mental Health Services Administration.

Saraga, M. Gholam-Rezaee, M., & Preisig, M. (2013). Symptoms, comorbidity, and clinical course of depression in immigrants: Putting psychopathology in context. *Journal of Affective Disorders*, *151*(2), 795–799. doi:10.1016/j.jad.2013.07.001

Scottish Government. (2018). New Scots: Refugee integration strategy 2018 to 2022. Retrieved from https://www.gov.scot/publications/new-scots-refugee-integration-strategy-2018-2022/

Shaw, I. (1996). *Evaluating in practice*. Bodmin: Arena.

Sijbrandij, M., Ceren, A., Bird, M., Bryant, R. A., Burchert, S., Carswell, K., … van Ittersum, L. (2017). Strengthening mental health care systems for Syrian refugees in Europe and the Middle East: Integrating scalable psychological interventions in eight countries. *European Journal of Psychotraumatology*, *8*(supl 2), 1388102. doi:10.1080/20008198.2017.1388102

Simpson, J. (2019). Navigating immigration law in a 'hostile environment': Implications for adult migrant language education. *Tesol Quarterly*, *54*(2), 488–511. doi:10.1002/tesq.558

Social Policy Research Centre. (2014). *New and emerging communities in Hounslow–mapping and needs assessment*. London: Social Policy Research Centre.

Spacey, M., & Thompson, N. (2021). Beyond individual trauma: Towards a multi-faceted trauma-informed restorative approach to youth justice that connects individual trauma with family reparation and recognition of bias and discrimination. British Journal of Community Justice. doi:10.48411/vcqn-0794

Stevenson, A., Kings, P., & Sterland, L. (2017). *Mapping ESOL provision in Greater London*. London: Learning and Work Institute.

Stevenson, J., & Willott, J. (2007). The aspiration and access to higher education of teenage refugees in the UK. *Compare: A Journal of Comparative Education*, *37*, 671–687. doi: 10.1080/03057920701582624

Sword, W. (1999). Accounting for presence of self: Reflections on doing qualitative research. *Qualitative Health Research*, *9*(2), 270–278. doi:10. 1177/104973299129121839

Taylor, K. (2009). Asylum seekers, refugees, and the politics of access to health care: A UK perspective. *British Journal of General Practice*, *59*(567), 765–772. doi:10.3399/bjgp09X472539

Thompson, N., & Nasimi, R. (2020). 'This place means freedom to me': Needs-based engagement with marginalized migrant Muslim women in London. *Community Development Journal*. doi:10.1093/cdj/bsaa029

Thompson, N., & Pihlaja, S. (2018). Temporary liberties and uncertain futures: Young female Muslims perceptions of life in England. *Journal of Youth Studies*, *21*(10), 1326–1343. doi:10.1080/13676261.2018.1468021

Umer, M., & Elliot, D. L. (2021). Being hopeful: Exploring the dynamics of post-traumatic growth and hope in refugees. *Journal of Refugee Studies*, *34*(1), 953–975. doi: 10.1093/jrs/fez002

UNHCR. (2019). *Desperate journeys: January–December 2018*. Geneva: UNHCR.

UNHCR. (2021a). Convention and protocol relating to the status of refugees: Text of the 1951 convention relating to the status of refugees. Retrieved from https://www.unhcr.org/3b66c2aa10.html

UNHCR. (2021b). Asylum in the UK. Retrieved from https://www.unhcr.org/uk/asylum-in-the-uk.html

UNHCR. (2021c). Global report 2020. Retrieved from https://www.unhcr.org/flagship-reports/globalreport/

UNHCR. (2021d). Refugee data finder. Retrieved from https://www.unhcr.org/refugee-statistics/

UNICEF. (2018). *All children in school and learning: Global initiative on out-of-school children-Afghanistan country study*. Geneva: UNICEF.

United Nations Office of the High Commissioner on Human Rights. (2018). Refugees and other migrants do not lose their rights by crossing borders. Retrieved from https://www.ohchr.org/EN/NewsEvents/Pages/RefugeesMigrantsDoNotLoseTheirRights.aspx

Uy, K. K., & Okubo, Y. (2018). Re-storying the trauma narrative: Fostering posttraumatic growth in Cambodian refugee women. *Women & Therapy*, *41*(3–4), 219–236. doi:10.1080/02703149.2018.1425025

Valtonen, K. (2004). From the margin to the mainstream: Conceptualizing refugee settlement processes. *Journal of Refugee Studies*, *17*(1), 70–96. doi:10.1093/jrs/17.1.70

van der Kolk, B. A. (2014). *The body keeps the score: Brain, mind, and body in the healing of trauma*. New York, NY: Viking.

Veroff, J., & DiStefano, A. (2002). Researching across difference–a reprise. *American Behavioral Scientist*, *45*(8), 1297–1307. doi:10.1177/0002764202045008013

Viruell-Fuentes, E. A., Miranda, P. Y., & Abdulrahim, S. (2012). More than culture: Structural racism, intersectionality theory and immigrant health. *Social Science & Medicine*, *75*(12), 2099–2106. doi:10.1016/j.socscimed.2011.12.037

von Werthern, M., Robjant, K., Chui, Z., Schon, R., Ottisova, L., Mason, C., & Katona, C. (2018). The impact of immigration detention on mental health: A systematic review. *BMC Psychiatry*, *18*, 1–19. doi:10.1186/s12888-018-1945-y

Vromans, L., Schweitzer, R. D., Brough, M., Correa-Velez, I., Murray, K., & Lenette, C. (2017). Contributions of loss events to loss distress and trauma symptoms in recently resettled refugee women at risk. *Journal of Loss & Trauma*, *22*(4), 357–370. doi:10.1080/15325024.2017.1296302

Wallerstein, N. (1992). Powerlessness, empowerment and health. Implications for health promotion programs. *American Journal of Health Promotion, 6*(3), 197–205. doi:10.4278/0890-1171-6.3.197

Ward, J. (2008). *ESOL: The context and issues*. Leicester: NIACE.

Wenham, A. (2015). Innovations in the measurement of youth work: The contribution of qualitative longitudinal methods. In N. Stanton (Ed.), *Innovation in youth work: Thinking in practice* (pp. 44–49). London: YMCA George Williams College.

Whittaker, A. (2012). *Research skills for social work* (2nd ed.). London: Sage.

Willott, J., & Stevenson, J. (2013). Attitudes to employment of professionally-qualified refugees in the UK. *International Migration, 51*(5), 120–132. doi:10.1111/imig.12038

Zulfacar, M. (1998). *Afghan immigrants in the USA and Germany. A comparative analysis of the use of ethnic social capital*. Münster: LIT Verlag.

INDEX

Acculturation, 9, 47
Action research, 21
   participatory action research,
      21–23
Afghanistan
   human rights activist in, 98–99
   humanitarian crisis, 2, 31
   refugee from, 3
Art therapy methods, 113–115
   art psychotherapy, 113
   dance movement psychotherapy,
      113
Aspiration
   aspirational empowerment, 133
   setting goals, 75–76
Asset-based community
      development (ABCD), 51
Assimilation, 46–47
Asylum applications, 30–31
Asylum seeker, 6–8, 30, 31, 33–36,
      47, 52, 113, 114
Austerity localism, 50

Body and mind' workshops, 119,
      124, 136
Bottom-up approach, 2–3
Brexit, 7–8, 46–47
British values', 47

Community Based Participatory
      Research (CBPR), 21
Community development, 43,
      129–130
   asset-based community
      development, 51
   asset-focused forms of, 44

with migrant and refugee
      women, 130–131
needs-based and asset-based
      approaches, 52
progressive localism, 50
top-down and bottom-up
      practice, 49–50
top-down assessment, 53
two-way integration, 46–47
Community work. *See* community
      development
Community-based approach, 2
Confidence, 60
   rebuilding, 98
Creative workshops, 123–124
Cultural relativism', 48
Culturally informed therapy, 115
Culture, 4–5, 15–16, 131

[Dis]empowerment, 34–37
Discourse
   academic, 6
   deficit-discourse, 50
   neoliberal, 52–53
Displacement, 6–7, 13, 109, 120

Employment, 34–37
Empowerment, 10–11, 93
   aspirational empowerment, 133
   journeys of change, 102–106
   long-term, 133–135
   stories of, 97–99
   sustainable empowerment,
      133–135
   sustainable levels of, 94
   tangible empowerment, 133

women's project in year three,
    94–95
workshops, 96–97
English for speakers of other
    languages (ESOL), 29, 36,
    71
Ethnicity, 5, 15–16, 126
Ethnographic approach, 16–17
European Union (EU), 7–8
Evaluation, 89, 97

Female genital mutilation (FGM),
    73, 75
Feminism, 4–5
Feminist intersectionality, 4–6
Feminist theory, 4–5
Freedom, 63–65

Gender, 5
    in Afghanistan, 32
    discrimination, 45, 47
    inequalities, 87
    in society, 4–5
Gendered racism, 5
Grassroots community project, 1–2
Grassroots practice and limits, 131
Grounding techniques, 120

Happiness, 59–60
Holistic practice, 109
Humanitarian crisis, 2

Insider research, 15–16, 19–20
Insider/outsider status, 23–27
Integration, 8–10
    grassroots practice and limits to,
        131
    isolation vs., 48–49
    two-way integration, 46–47
Interpretivism, 16
Interpretivist paradigm, 16–17
Intersectionality. See also Feminist
    intersectionality, 3–5
Islam. See Muslim
Isolation vs. integration, 48–49

Journey of change' model, 94

Knowledge and skills, 61–62
Learning English, 34, 37, 84–85
Literacy, 12, 29, 37, 39, 41
Localism
    austerity, 50
    progressive, 50
London
    Muslim university students in,
        46
    women's project in, 37, 72, 89
Long-term empowerment, 133–135
Longitudinal research
    qualitative longitudinal research,
        17

Mental health and trauma,
    135–136
Migrant communities
    movement and art therapy
        methods with, 113–115
    trauma-informed practice with,
        111–112
    women's experience of trauma,
        115–119
Migrant[s], 7–8, 15
    [dis]empowerment, 34–37
    asylum applications, 30–31
    employment, 34–37
    learning English, 34–37
    Muslim, 49
    people, 6–8
    and refugee groups, 29
    seeking assessment and support,
        33–34
    traumatic trajectories, 31–33
    women's project–cohort profile,
        37–41
Migration, 6
Movement therapy methods,
    113–115
Multi-culturalism, 9–10
Music therapy, 115
Muslim
    communities, 9, 45
    cultural identities, 8–9

UK Independence Party (UKIP),
   46–47
United Kingdom, Muslim women
   in, 44–46

Wellbeing, 59–60
Women's empowerment, 71
Women's project, 3–4, 55–56, 72,
   109
   age and family status, 38–39
   challenges, 66–67
   cohort profile, 37–41

countries of origin, 37–38
education and literacy levels,
   39–41
isolation towards integration,
   62–63
qualitative themes, 58–65
research data, 94
workshops, 57–58
in year one, 56
in year three, 94–95
Workshops, 57–58, 73, 75